Belongs to

Sandra Barr Boyd

(Mrs George Boyd V)

2016

PILGRIM

Pilgrim

A Biography of William Brewster

Mary B. Sherwood

Great Oak Press of Virginia
Falls Church, Virginia
1982

Library of Congress Cataloging in Publication Data

Sherwood, Mary B.
    Pilgrim.

        Bibliography: p.
        Includes index.
        1. Brewster, William, 1566 or 7-1644. 2. Massachusetts—History
—New Plymouth, 1620-1691. 3. Pilgrims (New Plymouth Colony)—
Biography. 4. Massachusetts—Biography. I. Title.
    F68.B84S53   973.2'2'0924 [B]   82-80574
    ISBN 0-9608234-0-9   AACR2

Printed in the United States of America
First Edition, 1982

*For my husband, Robert B. Sherwood; and
for our children, Elizabeth and Nicholas*

Contents

Preface

M ARY, QUEEN OF SCOTS and prisoner of the
English, drew a pair of red sleeves over her
slender hands and kneeled before the executioner's black-
draped block in the great hall of Fotheringhay Castle.

The executioner raised his axe and brought it down
twice. Mary Stuart was dead, but a third slice with the
axe completed the headsman's work.

The execution had been carried out in accordance with
the verdict of the special commission appointed to try
Mary for conspiring to kill Queen Elizabeth and seize
the throne of England, in accordance with the sentence
of Parliament, and in obedience to the death warrant
signed by Elizabeth.

The blows of the axe which took the life of the Queen
of Scots also ended the career of a distinguished English
diplomat and changed the direction of the life of a very
young man in the diplomat's service. The diplomat was
William Davison, a principal secretary of state. The
young man was William Brewster, and the new direction
led him to help found the colony of dissenters which they
called Plymouth, in the New World.

What a long, winding journey it was!

9

William Brewster is usually remembered in history as the good grey elder of the Pilgrim church. But first he was a student among radicals at Cambridge, a witness to the power plays of the Elizabethan Court, a post-master at Scrooby, a printer of forbidden books in Leyden, the Netherlands. He was a complicated man, and he was the single most important individual in the formation and development of the group of settlers known as the Pilgrims.

The Pilgrims are usually thought of "en masse," with the exceptions of William Bradford, who wrote their history, and of John Alden, Priscilla Mullins, and Myles Standish, immortalized by Longfellow.

I have tried to pluck William Brewster out of the group picture, to present him as an individual. In some ways this is possible only by recreating the background of the times and what went on around him. One can view the scenes that Brewster saw, share the experiences of which he was a part, and perhaps understand something of the man he was and why he acted as he did.

This is not a work of fiction. I have reported only what historians say actually happened, although sometimes it has been necessary to decide which of several versions is the most likely, in view of other facts. There are no fictitious characters, no conversations that contemporary writers did not record.

In general, I have used modern spelling but not changed the words in quoting from 16th and 17th century documents. Samuel Eliot Morison's excellent edition of William Bradford's history *Of Plymouth Plantation* is the source of all quotations from that history.

Spellings of names, as well as other words, varied wide-ly in this period. William Brewster spelled it "Brewster" in his own signature, although contemporary documents sometimes gave it as "Bruster."

Dates of the month are given in the "Old Style" used in England and her colonies until calendar revision in 1752. This means that a date in this book is ten days earlier than it would be in the "New Style" adopted in 1752. Under the "Old Style" system, each new year began on March 25, rather than January 1. Sometimes historians give a date occurring in January, February or March before 1752 two dates, as in February 8, 1620/21. This indicates that the people alive that February day considered that they were still living in 1620, but that a modern reader would think of the date as February 8, 1621. I have arbitrarily chosen January 1 as the first day of the year for this book, but continue to use the dates of the month as the Pilgrims did.

This is not another Pilgrim history. Bradford did that best himself, and the entire Pilgrim story is well researched and told in George F. Willison's *Saints and Strangers* (Reynal & Hitchcock, New York 1945).

Pilgrim is the story of one man and the world he saw.

Mary B. Sherwood
Falls Church, Virginia
March 1982

1 Down the Great North Road to London

THE GREAT NORTH ROAD from London to Scotland, as it ran in those days, cut through the village of Scrooby in the north of England. On one side of the old road was—and is—St. Wilfrid's church, where the faith has been preserved in changing fashion and in several structures since at least the 12th century.

On the other side of the old Great North Road, a few hundred yards back from the road, was Scrooby Manor, one of the palaces of the Archbishop of York, where Brewster's father, and later William Brewster himself served as bailiff, a sort of administrator for the estate.

The ground is flat between the church and the Manor site. The steeple of St. Wilfrid's is perfectly visible from the windows of a farmhouse which now stands on the palace land. A present-day church publication observes that the steeple looks from the distance like a sharpened pencil.

The existing church records do not go back far enough to include the date of William Brewster's birth or baptism. A bit of detective work, however, places his birth at about 1567. One arrives at this date thanks to the careful court record keeping of the Dutch. In 1609, Brewster

appeared as a witness in a civil suit in Leyden, and the
Dutch court records refer to him as "William Brewster,
Englishman, aged about 42 years."[1]

When William was about eight or nine years old, he
came to live in Scrooby Manor house, a huge, somewhat
decayed establishment over which his father (also named
William) presided as receiver and bailiff of the Manor.
Archbishop of York Edmund Grindal made the appointment, since the Manor was the Archbishop's residence
whenever he came to this area. A few months after ap-
pointing Brewster, Grindal became Archbishop of Canterbury, the highest church post in all England, and was
succeeded as Archbishop of York by Edwin Sandys, a
name that recurs repeatedly and benignly in the story of
William Brewster's life and the travels of the Pilgrims.

The post of bailiff and receiver paid 3 pounds 6s. 8d. a
year, which wasn't much even in the 16th century, but
the fringe benefits were appreciable. Brewster received
the use of the Manor seat and the fruits of its grounds.
He was also responsible for collecting manorial fees from
the tenants on the extensive grounds belonging to the
Manor. In minor disputes he acted as magistrate.[2]

Almost nothing is known of William Brewster, Sr.,
other than that he served in his post, apparently satisfac-
torily, until he died in 1590. His wife's name was
Prudence, the kind of name favored by Puritans, those
who would "purify" the Church of England by eliminat-
ing practices reminiscent of the Church of Rome. He was
apparently the sort of substantial citizen called upon to
administer a neighbor's will or to witness it. The late
Walter H. Burgess, a British writer and a Unitarian minister, discovered several examples of such service by
Brewster Senior. Burgess hoped to write a biography of
William Brewster of the Pilgrims to follow his excellent

biography of the Pilgrims' minister, *The Pastor of the Pilgrims, a Biography of John Robinson.*[3]

More recently, American Genealogist John G. Hunt, after a study of several 16th century English legal documents, has drawn some new conclusions about William Brewster's family background.

It follows this pattern, beginning with the grandfather of the William Brewster who sailed on the *Mayflower*:

> I. William Brewster, taxed in 1524 at Bently-cum-Arksey, and apparently married to Maude Man. Their sons were William, born about 1535, and Henry, vicar at Sutton-cum-Lound.
>
> II. William Brewster, born about 1535, married twice. His first wife was Mary (Smythe) Simkinson, widow of John Simkinson of Doncaster. Her father was William Smythe of Stainforth.[4]

Apparently the William who was to sail eventually on the *Mayflower* was the son of William and Mary (Smythe) Simkinson Brewster. Following Mary's death, her husband was married again, this time to the Prudence who was to survive him. The genealogist, Mr. Hunt, believes that three children were born to this marriage—James, who succeeded Henry Brewster as vicar at Sutton-cum-Lound; Prudence, who married Robert Peck; and John.[5]

Scrooby Manor must have been a marvelous place for a boy. The River Ryton flowed beside it. The Manor house itself had 40 rooms or so, and there were stables and outbuildings.

Splendid it had once been, but even by the time the Brewsters moved in, it must have been in need of more repair than it got. A hundred years later, in 1677, the historian Thoroton wrote of it, "Here within memory stood a very fair palace, a far greater house of receit and a better seat for provision than Southwell, and had attending to it the North Soke, consisting of very many towns thereabouts; it hath a fair park belonging to it. Archbishop Sandes caused it to be demised to his son Sir Samuel Sandes, since which the house hath been demolished almost to the ground.''[6]

In the days of its glory though, the house was the palace of the Archbishop of York when he was seeing to the work of the Church in this area. He had similar houses (Southwell was one) elsewhere in the North of England.

Scrooby Manor was also an occasional lodging for other persons high in the Court or the Church. The stories of such visits before William Brewster's time were told and retold in the village.

Margaret Tudor, daughter of King Henry VII, slept there one June night in 1503, while she was travelling north to become the bride of James IV of Scotland.

Cardinal Wolsey, after he had lost the favor of King Henry VIII, spent three months at Scrooby Manor in the summer of 1530, following a period at his other Manor house at Southwell. While at Scrooby, Wolsey was active, visiting parish churches in the area, saying mass in some, and inviting some members of the parish to share in the dinner he had brought with him. He died two months after leaving Scrooby for York.[7]

Henry VIII held a Privy Council meeting at the Manor in 1541. Doubtless he also took advantage of the hunting, since the red deer were plentiful then in the forests nearby and the King loved to hunt.

In the time of Henry VIII, this is the way Scrooby and its Manor house looked, according to John Leland, who held the unique post of Royal Antiquarian:

"In the mean townlet of Scrooby, I marked two things—the parish church, not big but very well builded; the second was a great manor place, standing within a moat and longing to the Archbishop of York; builded in two courts, whereof the first is very ample and all builded of timber, saving the front of the house that is of brick, to the which *ascenditur per gradus lapideos* [one ascends by stone steps]. The inner court building, as far as I marked, was of timber building, and was not in compass past the fourth part of the outer court."[8]

Within the Manor house were a chapel with a timber altar and a pair of organs, a dining hall "ceiled and dressed with wainscot," and a hall containing six tables. This painstaking inventory was reported by two visiting government officials.[9]

In short, it was undoubtedly the most imposing residence in the area, even in its latter-day decay.

In addition to his duties as overseer for the Archbishop, William Brewster, Sr., was also master of the Scrooby station of the Royal Post. The post was the Queen's post; the couriers who carried messages for the Queen to her officials in the North or to Scotland travelled over the Great North Road. Scrooby Manor was their official stopping place on the 24-mile stretch between Tuxford and Doncaster. The postmaster—more of an innkeeper than a postal official—was responsible for providing sleeping quarters for the couriers and for other official travelers. He also provided ale for their refreshment, food for their dinner, stables for their horses.

In return Mr. Brewster received a salary as postmaster of 30 pounds 8s. 44d. a year and the profit from his charge for food and beds. It was a comfortable living and his as long as he wanted it. It could have been his son's indefinitely too if he had not become a religious nonconformist.[10]

The Manor house would have been a fascinating spot for a young boy, with the opportunity to hear the travellers' tales of what was happening at the Court in London or wherever Queen Elizabeth might be. Such accounts were an introduction to the world beyond the flat horizons of Nottinghamshire and an invitation to explore it.

2 Cambridge and the Young Radicals

W HEN WILLIAM BREWSTER was about 13 years old, he left Scrooby to enroll at Cambridge University.

So many things about his early life are vague or missing, but this at least is certain. His name was entered in the records of Peterhouse College, Cambridge, on December 3, 1580, and he enrolled as a pensioner, one who could pay for his educational fees, rather than as a "sizar," a student who worked his way through college.[1]

Peterhouse is the oldest of the Cambridge colleges. It was founded in 1284 by Hugh de Balsham, Bishop of Ely. A figure of the Bishop appears in one of the stained glass windows of the hall of Peterhouse today, still presiding over scholars as they dine.[2]

The hall is still much as it was when William Brewster first saw it through a low doorway which still exists. The hall is a large room with a high ceiling, dark wooden paneling about ten feet up the walls, and furnished with long wooden tables and benches. It is the oldest surviving collegiate building in Cambridge, renovated but essentially as it was in 1580. The present lovely chapel of Peterhouse was built 50 years after Brewster left

Cambridge. During his time, the (still existing today) adjacent church of St. Mary the Less was used by Peterhouse for religious services.[3]

It was a long horseback ride from Scrooby to Cambridge, about 100 miles. Students from the same general area often rode to the university together, as much for safety as for companionship. Highway robbers were a threat, especially to students who were carrying with them the money they would need for an entire term. Perhaps William Brewster rode in company with the London-bound post. In the late fall, when he made his first trip, at least the trees had lost their leaves so there were fewer stretches of road where robbers might conceal themselves.

By the time William entered Cambridge he was proficient in Latin, which he learned in his local grammar school. Latin was essential, the opening wedge to all the professions—law, diplomacy, civil service. A merchant or the bailiff of a Manor like William's father would even need it in keeping his accounts. It was the language of diplomacy. Queen Elizabeth once carried on a denunciation of the Ambassador of Poland in fluent, furious Latin. Francis Bacon called Latin "the general language."[4]

A boy in grammar school could count on spending a large amount of his time between the ages of 7 or 8 to 14 or so translating Latin into English, or translating English back to Latin. William Brewster and his schoolmates, if their school followed the common pattern, competed against each other in conjugating Latin verbs and declining nouns.[5]

As soon as they mastered elementary Latin, the boys would be required to compose in it, such tasks as writing letters exhorting an imaginary reader to follow a certain course, or upbraiding him for what he had already done.

The boys had to carry on conversations in Latin, prepare orations and sometimes put on the plays of Terence and Plautus. Their reading would include Cicero, selected pieces from Ovid, Virgil, Sallust.[6]

A.L. Rowse, in *The England of Elizabeth* writes that by 1600 there were 360 grammar schools, founded in response to the great expansion in the middle ranks of society.[7]

At about the same time William Brewster was growing up in Scrooby, William Shakespeare was receiving his only formal education in the grammar school of Stratford-on-Avon.

A student in grammar school would have been in the classroom from 6 a.m. until 5:30 p.m. in the summer, and from 7 a.m. to 4:30 p.m. in the winter, with an interval midway through the day for dinner. Thursday afternoon was usually a holiday, and of course Sunday always was.[8]

England may have been a stratified society, but during the Tudor period the strata constantly shifted. The sons of "gentlemen" (except for the great nobility) attended the grammar schools along with the sons of yeomen. Generally the girls received what education they might get at the "pettie" schools, elementary schools where both little boys and girls learned to read and write.[9]

Wallace Notestein in *1603-1630 The English People on the Eve of Colonization* writes that "a few of the wise and useful in the days of the Stuarts were great-great grandsons of bondsmen."[10]

It was also easy to lose power or money. John Aubrey, the great gossipy biographer, tells of the son of the Bishop of Oxford, who "is run out of all, and goes begging up and down to gentlemen."[11]

However restricted society was to become later, there was opportunity for upward mobility in the last years of the 16th century. A thrifty yeoman could send his boy to the university, where he could study for the church, or prepare to be a schoolmaster, or even a lawyer or physician.[12]

For a boy from the country, Brewster must have found Cambridge exciting, stimulating and dangerous.

Lord Burghley (Sir William Cecil), Queen Elizabeth's First Secretary, was also the chancellor of Cambridge for nearly 40 years, and he kept a sharp eye on the behavior of undergraduates. In one directive he warned them not to use "very costly and disguised manner of apparel, and other attires unseemly for students in any kind of humane learning, but rather meet for riotous prodigals."[13]

More important, Cecil guided the university in the ways of the state religion of the Queen and kept extremists from tearing it apart.

Cambridge had been dangerously involved in the Church and State battles during the reign of King Henry VIII and afterward. After the death of Henry's short-lived heir, Edward VI, in 1553, the Duke of Northumberland proclaimed his own daughter-in-law, Lady Jane Grey, as Queen and led an army in pursuit of the rightful heir to the throne, Edward's sister Mary. Northumberland paused in Cambridge and secured the brief support of the university's Vice Chancellor Edwin Sandys. Desertions from Northumberland's army forced the Duke to abandon his hopeless cause. Both Northumberland and Sandys then proclaimed the accession of Queen Mary, too late for Northumberland and almost too late for Sandys. Both were taken to the Tower. Northumberland was executed, but Sandys was released, eventually to become Archbishop of York and William Brewster's Scrooby landlord.[14]

Following the accession of Elizabeth as Queen, the university flourished, and she expressed her pleasure in it by making a six-day visit in August 1564, 16 years before Brewster entered Peterhouse. By his time, her visit was a university legend. The Queen's long stay was an exhausting round of sermons, orations in Latin and Greek, and plays. The Queen, escorted through the colleges, kept up a conversation in Latin with her hosts. Finally, exhausted, she cancelled her attendance at a performance of Sophocles' *Ajax*.[15]

It is frustrating that there is absolutely no indication of what William Brewster looked like, either at Cambridge or at any other time in his long life. William Bradford never mentions it in his history. The portrayal of Brewster in paintings of the Pilgrims is pure imagination.

The other young men at the university would have liked him. All his life Brewster drew many friends, attracted by his pleasant, cheerful disposition and his integrity. He was unassuming, sympathetic toward those in trouble, faithful to his friends and discreet.

Although he was only 13 or so on entering Peterhouse College, this entering age was not unusual. Craig R. Thompson in *Universities in Tudor England* writes that 15 was the average university entering age during the 16th century. The brilliant, ambitious Francis Bacon was only 12 when he and his 15-year-old brother entered Trinity College in 1573; by Brewster's time Francis Bacon had left Cambridge after spending three years there, not taking a degree. Later on Bacon wrote that many scholars came "too soon and too unripe" to the universities. As a result, he said, teaching was superficial "as fitteth indeed to the capacity of children."[16]

A dazzling young man, Robert Devereux, Earl of Essex, whose life later tangled with Bacon's, was a familiar figure at Cambridge during Brewster's school days. Essex was a student at Trinity College when Brewster was a student at Peterhouse, and they must have been almost the same age. Essex was only 14 when he received the Master of Arts degree in 1581 and left Cambridge for the brief future that made him the Queen's favorite when he was 21 and led to his execution at the age of 33.

Even during the Cambridge years, Essex would have been recognized by all, both for his title and for his striking appearance. Essex was tall and handsome. He walked with his head thrust forward, with a striding gait; his eyes were black and his hair auburn. Rudeness and sullenness when thwarted, an observer noted, were at times offset by an extraordinary sweetness.

A book that Bacon wrote about Essex was in William Brewster's library at the time of Brewster's death in America more than 60 years after their Cambridge days.

Other Cambridge students would also have been aware of the presence of witty John Harington, who was Queen Elizabeth's godson. He was a 19-year-old student at King's College, Cambridge, the year that Brewster enrolled.

Another Cambridge contemporary was Christopher (Kit) Marlowe, son of a shoemaker from Canterbury. Marlowe was a pensioner of Benet College. A few years after leaving Cambridge he was a successful playwright (*Tamburlaine the Great, The Tragical History of Doctor Faustus* and others). He died in 1593 at the age of 29, reportedly killed during a quarrel over the bill in a tavern in Deptford. In one scene of *Tamburlaine the Great, Part I* Marlowe is perhaps reflecting something of his own period's social mobility. The heroine, Zenocrate, addresses Tamburlaine as "My Lord," adding, "for so you do import." And Tamburlaine responds, "I am a lord, for so my deeds shall prove; and yet a shepherd by my parentage."[17]

A Peterhouse student who enrolled the same day that Brewster did was John Penry. Peterhouse only had about 100 students, so Brewster surely knew John Penry, a clever young Welshman, quick with a jest and not at all awed by pompous authority. He probably knew Penry's close friend, John Greenwood, a student at Corpus Christi College.[18]

Both Penry and Greenwood were to die a few years later on the gallows for crimes related to resistance to the state religion. Both were active in organizing a Separatist congregation in London a few years after leaving Cambridge. Greenwood and another Separatist, Henry Barrow—who had also been a Cambridge student somewhat earlier—were hanged in 1593 for sedition, specifically for publishing pamphlets critical of the Established Church. One of them, *A Briefe Discoverie of the False Church*, was printed in Holland and smuggled back into England. In 1620 William Brewster took a copy of it with him to Plymouth.[19]

A few weeks after Greenwood and Barrow were hanged in 1593, Penry too was brought to trial, condemned, hanged, drawn and quartered. He was accused of publishing the series of tracts signed "Martin Marprelate," witty, ironic writings critical of the English clergy. The authorship of the articles has never been determined.[20]

There were other religious radicals at Cambridge during Brewster's time. One of them was Francis Johnson, a fellow at Christ's College, who later became a clergyman. As a clergyman, Johnson was in favor of purifying the church, but at first he opposed Separatism. In 1590 he helped seize Henry Barrow's tracts. However he

saved a couple of copies, read one, and was converted
to the cause of Separatism. Johnson visited Barrow in
prison, resigned his church position and joined the Separatists. Still later his path crossed Brewster's in Amsterdam; Johnson then was pastor of the Separatists there
known as the Ancient Brethren.[21]

Another fellow at Christ's College in the early 1580's
was William Perkins, who also became a preacher. Brewster reprinted a volume of Perkins' sermons in a print
shop at Leyden, the Netherlands, and took several volumes of the sermons with him to Plymouth.[22]

At Leyden Brewster also printed the writings of another former Cambridge schoolmate, John Udall, who
was at Trinity College when Brewster was at Peterhouse.
Udall's "seditious" writings sent him to prison. Although
he was condemned to death in 1588, the sentence was
never carried out. He died in prison four years later.
Udall was also suspected of writing the Marprelate
works.[23]

Brewster would have known or heard about all these
young men. He was influenced by those who were advo-
cating Separatism in the church. Cambridge must have
been a lively place. Milton, assessing his own Cambridge
days some 50 years farther on, complained that the students were drawn into fathomless depths of controversy
when they were expecting worthy and delightful knowledge. Whatever Brewster's expectations, he certainly
found controversy.

The regimen was rather spartan. A college bell wak-
ened university students at 5 a.m. in the summer and at
6 in the winter. Breakfast was light, sometimes including
a glass of beer; dinner was at 11 a.m. and supper at 5
p.m., served in the college's great hall. Five or six students were assigned to the guidance of one fellow, and all

slept in one room. They studied in small adjacent rooms.[24]

The lecture halls were unheated—and the later part of the 16th century and the first part of the next were unusually cold. They were known as the Little Ice Age.

How deeply Brewster was drawn into the controversies that involved so many of his contemporaries is unclear. Bradford writes simply that Brewster "spent some small time at Cambridge, and then being first seasoned with the seeds of grace and virtue, he went to the Court and served that religious and godly gentleman Mr. Davison, divers years when he was Secretary of State."[25]

In short, for the first few years after Brewster left Cambridge, he was a member of the establishment.

3 The Court of the Glorious Queen

THE COURT OF QUEEN ELIZABETH the First still glows, 400 years later, with a sort of persisting radiation. Biographies, plays, operas, historical novels, films continue to be produced about her although Queen Elizabeth has rested in her burial vault in Westminster Abbey since 1603.

If even the 400-year-old memory continues to hold fascination, the Court was irresistible to many English men and women of the late 16th century. The daring, the ambitious, the lovers of intrigue and excitement were often more conspicuous than were the more conservative public officials who served there too. The Court was highly competitive; favors were gained or lost, "new men" in many cases rose from relative obscurity to replace earlier favorites who had fallen from grace.

In the center was the Queen. In her gold-embroidered gowns, with pearls in her hair or falling in ropes to her waist, Elizabeth was Gloriana, her subjects' ideal of beauty and grace. She was the most astute figure of her time, the most intelligent ruler that England had ever had. The poet-soldier Sir Philip Sidney wrote, "Her inward worth all outward show transcends."

The men of her Court shone only when she allowed

29

them to reflect her glory, and the women were never permitted to shine at all. At her side for most of her life was
Sir William Cecil, later Lord Burghley, her principal minister and the most selfless of all her public servants.
Closer to her personally was Robert Dudley, whom she
made Earl of Leicester, her childhood playmate, her lov-
er, and often the target of her disapproval for his personal
or political indiscretions.

Her Secretary Sir Francis Walsingham set up an effi-
cient espionage network throughout the courts of Europe
and in England as well, with the twin purposes of guarding against threats to the throne of England and guarding
against threats to restore the power of the Church of
Rome in England.

The circle around the Queen included the other principal advisors of her Privy Council, ambassadors from
European courts, certain courtiers whose fame rested
mainly on their dancing or their social attentions to the
Queen, the Queen's ladies in waiting, and 500 bureau-
crats to carry out the country's business.

At the very outer orbit for a period of between three
and five years was the former Cambridge student, William Brewster.

Even the outer orbit had its excitement. The Queen
was no isolated chief of state; her chief aim was to win
and retain the love of her subjects, and one device to do
this was to make herself highly visible in a setting of
splendor, of Majesty.

Brewster apparently left Cambridge without taking a
degree. There is no record of it. A B.A. degree was customarily but not invariably awarded after four years of
study. In 1583, about the time Brewster left the university, Cambridge conferred 277 B.A. degrees, the highest number granted in any year of the 16th century.[1]

William Brewster's employer at Court, William Davison, had served with some distinction on a number of diplomatic missions and his star was still rising.

The Queen's favorite, Robert Dudley, the Earl of Leicester, who was a cousin of Davison's, wrote in 1577 to him at Antwerp, where Davison was serving as an English envoy, "I am glad to find your service so agreeable not only to those there, but Her Majesty here concerning so good an opinion of you that you have cause to rejoice."[2]

By 1579 Davison had gained "so high a reputation at Court that he was employed on every object which required nice and difficult management." (The assessment was that of the early 19th century biographer Sir Nicholas H. Nicolas, who wrote a life of Davison.)[3]

Bradford in his Plymouth history refers to Davison as "that religious and godly gentleman," which was the aspect of his character that Brewster apparently considered most important in telling Bradford about Davison, or at least the aspect that Bradford himself considered most significant.

There are no clues as to how the Cambridge student met the diplomat. Perhaps at the Manor house in Scrooby in the course of one of Davison's frequent official missions up the Great North Road to Scotland? Perhaps through the intervention of Archbishop Sandys, the Manor landlord, or through Sandys' son Edwin? The Sandys family helped the Brewsters on many occasions.

Neither is there any way of determining the date on which Brewster, a minor employee, entered Davison's service, except that it was before the autumn of 1585 when Brewster accompanied Davison to the Netherlands. Bradford, in referring to Brewster's employment with Davison, wrote at some length about that

Netherlands experience and of time spent at Court. He does not refer to Davison's diplomatic missions in Scotland in 1582 through September 1584, so it is probable that Brewster had not joined his service until after the diplomat's duties in Scotland had ended.

In 1585, Brewster was about 18 years of age, and Davison was about 44. The extent of Brewster's responsibility is cloudy; he probably filled a minor clerical position, at least at the beginning, certainly less than the "private secretary" role that some writers have assigned him.

The employment was satisfactory to both. Bradford writes that Davison found Brewster "so discreet and faithful as he trusted him above all other that were about him, and only employed him in all matters of greatest trust and secrecy; he esteemed him rather as a son than a servant, and for his wisdom and godliness, in private he would converse with him more like a friend and familiar than a master."[4]

Through the archaic language, it is possible to see the touching picture of a young man thrilled by confidential disclosures about the exciting events of his times and of a professional diplomat enjoying the role of raconteur and teacher.

An observer later described Davison as "a handsome man with a grave expression of countenance and possessed of a fine voice; his temper was peculiarly mild and benign, his manners urbane and persuasive. . . . the sweetest man living."[5] (Sweet was used at the time as a synonym for extremely pleasant or likeable.)

Also a member of Davison's staff at about the time Brewster entered his employment was young George Cranmer, grandnephew of Archbishop Thomas Cranmer. The Archbishop helped Henry VIII marry Anne Boleyn, and was burned at the stake when Mary Tudor was

Queen. George Cranmer, who was a little older than William Brewster, had been a student at Oxford with Edwin Sandys, the son of the Brewsters' Scrooby Manor landlord. After they left Oxford, George and Edwin spent three years travelling on the continent together. Returning to England, George joined Davison's staff.[6]

Davison himself had been only 25 years old when he was sent to Scotland on his first important assignment. He accompanied his own superior at that time, Sir Henry Killegrew, as secretary to the mission dispatched by Queen Elizabeth to congratulate Mary, the Queen of Scots, on the birth of her son James.[7]

Ironically, the eventual fate of the Queen of Scots ended the diplomatic career of Davison.

But in 1585 his career seemed secure. The early 1580's saw increasing dangers to England from without, as well as personal peril to Queen Elizabeth. Both dangers resulted in restraints on freedom of action and speech in England.

In Spain Philip II schemed to bring England under his power. Philip had been the husband of Elizabeth's predecessor, her half-sister, Queen Mary. After Mary's death and Elizabeth's accession, he had been one of the many suitors for the hand of Elizabeth, and one of the many whose interest she had managed to keep during the time she dallied with the marriage proposals she never accepted.

Spain claimed sovereignty over the Low Countries, areas of the present Belgium and the Netherlands. A revolt by the Dutch under William of Orange challenged the power of Spain. France was tempted to intervene with the hope of weakening Spain, thus increasing the power of France. Uncontested superiority of either the Spanish or French in the Low Countries would have provided a staging area which either could use for an invasion of England.

Elizabeth sometimes aided the French against the Spanish in the Netherlands, sometimes gave money and arms to support the Dutch.

Another danger to England was the possibility that a Spanish force could first land in Ireland and thus be poised for the shorter final thrust at England itself. England had already begun the centuries-long, disastrous policy of attempting to subjugate the Irish, and rebellion there, then as later, was always brewing.

Equally dangerous to the security of England and to the life of Queen Elizabeth was the web of plots known under the euphemism of the "Enterprise of England." The Enterprise was a plan to assassinate Elizabeth, place Mary Queen of Scots on the throne of England, and restore the Catholic religion. The plotters were mostly English Catholic refugees living in Europe and sympathizers still in England, and they were aided by the Church of Rome. The Papal Secretary wrote in December 1580, "Since that guilty woman of England rules over two such noble kingdoms of Christendom and is the cause of so much injury to the Catholic faith and loss of so many million souls, there is no doubt that whoever sends her out of the world with the pious intention of doing God service, not only does not sin but gains merit."[8]

The Enterprise plotters counted on a Catholic uprising in England and on English Catholics' support of a Spanish invasion, but the greatest number of English Catholics were faithful both to their religion and to their Queen, who had tolerated their private exercise of their faith. However Catholic priests, sent secretly from the continent to England in the early 1580's, were hunted down and some were executed.

This was the atmosphere when William Brewster entered Court service in about 1584, perhaps a year earlier or later.

He served Mr. Davison "at Court," which meant that Brewster and his employer were part of the entourage which moved when the Queen moved from one of her palaces to another. There were 14 major palaces in regular use, as well as some smaller establishments where she might stay a night or so.[9]

She nearly took over another establishment—the Manor house at Scrooby.

In 1582, during William Brewster's Cambridge days, the Queen planned to let the Earl of Leicester lease the Manor, probably to use as a hunting lodge. However Archbishop Sandys was able to persuade her not to do it. He pleaded that it would be a serious deprivation, both to himself and the bishopric, that he had recently spent a good deal of money in repairs and improvements. The loss of the Manor, he wrote to the Queen, would be "too much, most gracious sovereign—too much to pull from a bishopric inferior to many in revenue, but superior in charge and countenance."[10]

Before the Queen could change her mind again, the Archbishop leased the Manor, two parks, mills and a forest to his oldest son, Sir Samuel Sandys. William Brewster, Sr., continued to reside at the Manor house as its bailiff and postmaster.[11]

At the time the younger William Brewster joined William Davison's staff, Davison was deep in negotiations to provide English military aid to the Dutch rebelling against Spanish occupation.

Queen Elizabeth was nearly 52 years of age in the summer of 1585 when the final decisions to aid the Dutch were made. She would soon celebrate the 27th year of her accession to the throne. During all that time she schemed to keep her country free from war, especially war on English soil. This policy was occasionally stretched, so far that Elizabeth's determination of "No war!" can be debated by historians. But in her own time, up to 1585, the policy had met her own definition of "no war," and that is what mattered. True, she had sent troops to Scotland early in her reign to help Scottish rebels expel French troops. True, she had sent a disastrous expedition to Le Havre in an attempt to wrest former English territories away from the French. True, she permitted her privateers to commit acts of piracy against Spanish ships. True, she had sent money to support both French and Dutch troops in their struggle with the Spanish rulers of the Netherlands.

But these actions she considered part of the defense of England.

She took pride, she said in a 1570 communication to her subjects, that in her reign there had been no needless foreign wars with their great cost, although she had been forced to incur some expenses in defending the country against intended invasions.[12]

Of Elizabeth's vacillating policy in the Netherlands, 19th century historian J.A. Froude wrote, "She dipped into the whirlpool and drew out of it, she hung on the edge and promised and broke her promises, and sent help to France and Flanders and denied having sent it."[13]

Davison, participating in negotiations for the Alliance which would formally commit English troops to service in the Netherlands, had undertaken several earlier missions there. He certainly told young Brewster something about the earlier assignments during the times when, as Bradford told it, "he would converse with him more like a friend and familiar than a master."[14] Even as a master, he would have briefed his subordinate on what to expect during the journey that both were to undertake.

During an assignment in 1576 following the death of the Spanish governor of the Low Countries, Davison was instructed to call upon both Spanish and Dutch to cease fire and begin negotiations for peace. The English threatened to join forces against whichever side refused. Neither side apparently took the threat seriously and there was no peace.[15]

Then and on later assignments, Davison was responsible for obtaining for Elizabeth information on conditions in the Netherlands which would help her determine how to act on applications for help made by the strong Dutch leader, William Prince of Orange.

Davison's 1576 mission was satisfactory to the Queen.

In July 1577 she sent Davison to Antwerp as her resident agent and in August diverted him briefly to Namur, which the new Spanish Governor of the Low Countries had seized, to observe further developments.[16]

This time Davison was instructed to tell William of Orange that the Queen would be sympathetic to a Dutch request for assistance.[17]

Intermittently Elizabeth furnished the Dutch rebels with money for arms and troops, but she insisted on security for her loans. In May 1579 Davison sailed for England with jewels furnished as pawns for English loans.[18]

The situation in the Low Countries worsened when William of Orange was assassinated in July 1584.

A few months later the Queen's Privy Council recommended that she send a "wise person" to the Low Countries to find out whether France was committed to assist the Dutch, and if not, to offer English help. The "wise person" selected was William Davison, who was also instructed to determine how much aid the Dutch would need and the extent of their resources.[19]

Brewster may have been on Davison's staff by this time and may have accompanied him on this mission to the Netherlands, as well as the journey he made a year later.

In 1584 the Dutch were trying to determine whether the English or the French would be more likely to furnish aid. At the same time Davison was discussing terms of English aid with Dutch officials in the Netherlands, Dutch envoys in Paris were also exploring the possibilities of future French aid. Prospects of more French assistance grew dim. Queen Elizabeth, informed of this by her agent in Paris, wrote to Davison, instructing him "to nourish in them [the Dutch] underhand some hope— as a thing proceeding from himself—that though France should reject them, yet she would not abandon them."[20]

Davison returned to England in compliance with the Queen's orders of April 1585 and remained there during negotiations with envoys sent to England by the Netherlands.

William Brewster, if not already a member of Davison's staff during the 1584-85 Netherlands mission, was surely his employee after Davison's return to England.

Brewster may have watched the arrival of the Netherlands Commissioners for their first audience with the Queen at Greenwich Palace in July 1585. They arrived in royal barges, to be welcomed by the Queen in a stately ceremony in her presence chamber, which was hung with Gobelin tapestry. The Queen wore a small gold crown; her red hair glittered with diamonds and emeralds. Fringes of pearls as large as beans decorated her satin and velvet garments. Her Councillors in their robes of state, as well as fifty gentlemen pensioners with gilt battle axes, stood beside the throne.[21]

The spokesman for the Dutch envoys expressed gratitude for the Queen's kindnesses and spoke highly of Davison's "good offices" extended after the death of the Prince of Orange.

The Dutch offered the Queen sovereignty over the Provinces under their control, as they had done before and were to do again. She consistently refused these offers.

Negotiations proceeded for several weeks, mostly in London, and in the final stages moved to one of Elizabeth's most ornate palaces, Nonsuch, a day's ride from London. William Brewster, used to Scrooby Manor's decaying timbers and Cambridge's medieval austerity, would have found Nonsuch dazzling indeed, if he was present during the envoys' visit there. Nonsuch meant literally that there was no other such building. It sparkled with gilt and white stucco; it bristled with statues of heraldic beasts, Roman emperors, characters from classical mythology and allegorical creatures. The palace is gone now, but it was then in the height of its splendor.[22]

Within the palace Dutch emissaries met with the Queen and her Councillors for a final determination of how far Elizabeth was willing to go in support of the Dutch rebellion.

By August 12, 1585, the Treaty of Alliance was concluded. Elizabeth formally committed English troops to be sent to the Low Countries. As the King of Sweden put it, "Queen Elizabeth has now taken the diadem from her head and ventured it upon the doubtful chance of war."[23]

Almost immediately the "chance" appeared still more doubtful, as news of the fall of Antwerp to the Spanish on August 7 was carried across the English channel. By August 12 Sir John Norris, a veteran of service in the

Low Countries, was named to command the English troops. Davison was ordered to the Low Countries to carry out the terms of the Alliance, leaving within days with the first military contingent in a situation of urgency.

The Queen told the Dutch people that she was sending them "our faithful and well-beloved Davison to represent to you how much we have your affairs at heart, and to say that we are determined to forget nothing that may be necessary to your preservation."[24]

William Brewster was a member of Davison's party.

Davison's immediate mission was to receive formally, in the Queen's name, authority over two Dutch towns and a fortress which the Dutch reluctantly agreed to give as security for the Queen's promise to send troops and horses and money to maintain them.

She would furnish this assistance, Lord Burghley told the Dutch negotiators, on the condition that she be "repaid to the last farthing when the war is over and until that period must have solid pledges in the shape of a town in each province."[25]

The towns pledged as security, referred to as the Cautionary Towns, were the ports of Flushing and Brill. The fortress of Ramikins was also pledged.

The English party disembarked in Flushing, then traveled to the Hague, where Davison met with Dutch officials on the implementation of the agreements. According to his instructions from Queen Elizabeth, Davison then visited each of the Cautionary Towns to receive possession of them in the Queen's name, symbolized by accepting the keys of the city. The keys were to be retained by the English official in temporary possession. In the Brill, Davison received the keys and transmitted them to Henry Norris, who would remain there.

In Flushing, however, Davison not only received the keys of the city but retained them, as he was himself ordered to take over the civil government and be in formal command of its fortifications, until the arrival of its future governor. Flushing guarded the principal approach to the Netherlands from the sea.[26]

It was now mid-October, and Brewster had for nearly two months been an observer and minor participant in Elizabethan England's only major foreign military adventure on land.

The actual transfer to Davison of the port of Flushing was attended with considerable ceremony. In the presence of the young Prince Maurice, son of the recently assassinated Prince of Orange, and of the dashing Count Hohenlo, General-in-Chief of the Dutch army, the English troops, marching from their quarters, filed into the town's principal church. There they swore an oath of fidelity to the present trust, then marched to the fortifications. The Dutch troops retired from the fortifications, transferring their responsibility to the English. The keys were handed to Davison as a token of the possession.[27]

Davison "kept them some time," according to Bradford's account. And, conscious of the thrill that handling the ornate keys would bring to his junior clerk, Davison asked Brewster to keep the keys in his own custody.[28]

It was a thrill indeed. Brewster put them under his pillow that night and slept with his head resting above this symbol of the Queen's authority. Years later he told Bradford about it.

Religion was an important factor in the Dutch rebellion, as it was in most other aspects of European affairs of the time. The English Protestants sympathized with the Dutch Protestants, but Queen Elizabeth would never have embarked on a religious war. Her motives were nationalistic, to prevent Spain from securing enough power to attack England.

In any event the Dutch Protestants' beliefs were too much like her own English Puritans' to please her. Elizabeth consistently resisted the Puritans' desire for further reforms in the church. Both Davison and his superior, Secretary Walsingham, were zealous Puritans, so the religious aspect of the Dutch revolt had considerable importance to them, as well as to Brewster. Brewster was only a few years out of Cambridge, where religion had been a primary subject of controversy.

Back at the Court in England, Robert Dudley, Earl of Leicester, was preparing to assume authority over all the English forces in the Netherlands—if Queen Elizabeth would let him. Leicester wanted to go; it was a position of greater responsibility than he had ever been allowed, and Leicester coveted power. The Dutch wanted him. The assassination of the Prince of Orange had deprived them of their popular leader, and Leicester, as a symbol of the new English support, would be of tremendous psychological value. His closeness to the Queen would signify that she was resolute in her commitment.

But she really did not want him to go. Elizabeth never liked to see him away from her side, even though she was still furious with him for his secret marriage to Lettice Knollys, recent widow of the first Earl of Essex. Elizabeth detested Lettice and would not permit her presence at Court, although Leicester himself was eventually welcomed back, following an initial period of banishment when the secret marriage was disclosed.

The Queen almost made up her mind at one point to send Leicester immediately. However she discovered that Lettice was planning to accompany him to the

Netherlands, presumably in the semi-regal style she was affecting in London.

An account of Lettice driving through London at about this time reads: "She rides through Cheapside drawn by four milk-white steeds with four footmen in black velvet jackets and silver bars on their backs and breasts, two knights and thirty gentlemen before her, so that it might be supposed to be the Queen or some foreign Prince or ambassador."[29]

Elizabeth would not countenance competition from anyone, particularly Lettice.

She withdrew permission to Leicester to depart. In early September Davison received a letter from Secretary Walsingham, telling him, "I see not her Majesty disposed to use the services of the Earl of Leicester. There is great offense taken in the carrying down of his lady."[30] Lettice had just left their country home at Kenilworth to take up a conspicuous residence at Leicester House on the Strand in London.

Leicester's appointment was re-instated though, and after several months of vacillation on the Queen's part about the actual setting of a departure date, he left Harwich for the Netherlands with his entourage on December 8, 1585. He had used the fall months not only to win back the Queen's good graces, but to outfit his expedition. He resented the Queen's well-known parsimony, writing to Burghley, "For if her Majesty be not persuaded and fully resolved that the cause is of other importance than, as it were, to make a show and become only a scarecrow, it were better never to enter into it." To supplement what Elizabeth was willing to furnish, Leicester mortgaged part of his property to her for funds which he used to equip the expedition he was undertaking in her name.[31]

On a windy, cold November day, Sir Philip Sidney, the brilliant, gentle poet-soldier, arrived to serve as the permanent Governor of Flushing and took over the custody of the keys that Brewster had briefly held for Davison. Lord Burghley's eldest son, Thomas Cecil, was named Governor of Brill.

Finally in December Leicester landed, attended by an impressive show of force. In his early fifties he was still a handsome man, tall and commanding, although his increasing years had also increased his weight, reddened his face, greyed his hair, and made it recede. His clothes were magnificent—satins and feathers, a velvet toque on his head, jewels in his ears.

Davison and presumably Brewster witnessed much of Leicester's triumphal procession through the Low Countries.

No one could miss one member of the party, the tall, swaggering figure of the 18-year-old Earl of Essex, stepson to Leicester and son of the controversial Lettice. The young man had the title of General of the Horse. William Brewster once again saw the handsome Earl who had been a Cambridge student four years earlier.

Leicester and his party expected to be and were treated royally. Arriving at Flushing, they were greeted with shouts of welcome, banners waving, ringing of bells and cannon salutes.

Davison and Brewster were evidently attached to some of the travels of the Leicester entourage, which took on the complexion of a triumphal procession, with a ceremony at the church in Flushing, a banquet following it, a military review at Middleburg, and in the Hague seven days of banqueting and other forms of hospitality extended by the Dutch and then reciprocated by Leicester. After further triumphal receptions in Dort, Rotterdam, and Delft, he returned to the Hague and established his headquarters, more like a royal establishment than a military base.[32]

Davison's services were satisfactory to Leicester. At some point, probably shortly after Leicester's arrival, Davison was called back to London to report on developments in the Netherlands. Leicester wrote to Burghley, "You shall find him [Davison] as sufficiently able to deliver the whole state of this country as any man that ever was in it, acquainted with all sorts here that are men of dealing."[33]

Leicester praised Davison's "credit with all the chief sort," as well as his reputation for keeping "a very good table." He urged the quick return of Davison to the Hague, "for I know not almost how to do without him."[34] Davison was promptly sent back to the Netherlands.

In January the Leicester entourage visited Leyden, the pleasant Dutch city where William Brewster was to find asylum more than twenty years later. Leyden staged a drama for the English forces, depicting events in the Spanish siege of Leyden and its eventual relief eleven years earlier.

On January 25, 1586, the Earl of Leicester, who had been commissioned by the Queen as her Lieutenant-General-in-Chief in the Low Countries, accepted from the Dutch a new title—Supreme Governor-General of the United Provinces. The Dutch invested him with nearly absolute authority, under Elizabeth.

He should have known better.

For a long time the Dutch had persistently begged Queen Elizabeth to take over the sovereignty of the Low Countries. She firmly refused, knowing that this would unnecessarily offend the King of Spain, who claimed sovereignty by inheritance. She was helping the Dutch, she emphasized, not for the purpose of taking them from their lawful sovereign, the King of Spain, but only to protect the rights of the Dutch to civil and religious freedom. Further, she had privately commanded Leicester not to accept any similar offer made to him.[35]

Davison knew how she felt about the Dutch sovereignty matter. Leicester surely knew how she felt and remembered her private commands to him, but he dared to presume that a *fait accompli* and his personal charms would persuade the Queen to overlook a decision she would have vetoed.

He was wrong.

Leicester sent Davison back to England with the impossible assignment of explaining to the Queen why Leicester had accepted this new title.

Before Davison embarked for England, the Dutch presented him with a gold chain in honor of his services, in still another of the ceremonies held in recognition of English aid and in encouragement of its continuance. Davison committed the chain to Brewster's keeping for the journey home.

They started their return trip on February 5, eleven days after Leicester's investiture ceremony in the banqueting hall of the ancient palace in the Hague. Winter winds and rough seas kept their ship from leaving the port of Brill for another five or six days. Finally the weather improved, and they sailed for England. Davison would never see Holland again. Brewster would be a refugee from England when he came again to Holland.

The crossing was uneventful. Davison wrote to Leicester from London that, after the delay for more favorable weather, "The Friday following I put in the seas, and by God's goodness had so happy a passage, as the next morning, by ten or eleven o'clock, we anchored at the Recolvers, within Margate, and the same night, about midnight, came to Gravesend, and from thence immediately with the tide hither, where I arrived the next morning early."[36]

It was Sunday morning.

William Brewster returned to his native land in splendor. Davison "commanded" Brewster to wear the gold chain awarded to Davison by the Netherlands as the party rode from the landing through London. Perhaps they felt it a continuation of the triumphal processions across the Dutch countryside.

The triumph was short-lived. Brewster probably expected, and Davison at least hoped, that the Queen would have a few words of commendation for the diplomat's performance during the delicate six-month mission in the Netherlands.

She agreed to receive him on the same day he arrived, and was waiting for him a few hours later in the inner drawing room of Greenwich Palace, one of her grandest palaces, set among fine gardens on the bank of the Thames. Greenwich guarded the approach to London by water.

Before the interview, Secretary Walsingham warned Davison that the Queen had already been told of Leicester's appointment and that she was furious.

The first part of the audience with the Queen was, Davison wrote later, "exceedingly sharp, not only against his Lordship [Leicester], for presuming so far without her privity and consent, and against her express commands; but also against me for not dissuading him and opposing myself to it."[37]

She demanded, how dared my Lord of Leicester accept the governorship against her express command, in contempt of her, and as if her consent had been nothing worth, or the thing no way concerning her?[38]

The Earl had accepted this title from the Dutch?

Very well, he must renounce it, publicly, on the very spot where he had been invested with it.

Davison was aghast. A public renunciation would not only humiliate Leicester in the eyes of both Dutch and English; it would be an insult to the Dutch. The occasion was quite a challenge to Davison's diplomatic skill.

The Queen determined to send Sir Thomas Heneage to the Low Countries to deliver to Leicester her command for a public renunciation. Fortunately, she hesitated, as she often did, to take final action until she had thought about it further.

Davison was carrying a letter to the Queen from Leicester and he tried to present it to her. She refused to receive it. The interview ended, and Davison went away appalled at the disastrous reception of his mission.

The next day he requested another interview, and rather surprisingly, he was received by the Queen. This time he pleaded with her with tears in his eyes.

Writing to Leicester following the interview, Davison said that he "besought her to be better advised, laying before her the dishonourable, shameful and dangerous effects of so unhappy a message, which would be utter ruin to the cause, and her own dishonour and undoing."[39]

The Queen was not mollified. Again Davison proffered the letter from Leicester. This time the Queen broke the seal and read a few words, then thrust it into her pocket, to read at leisure, Davison hoped.

It was the absolute title of Governor-General—and the way the Dutch were addressing Leicester as "Excellency"—that the Queen found completely unacceptable. He might have had the substance if he would have forborne the title, she said. Davison questioned whether the King of Spain would distinguish "between the name and the thing."[40]

The Queen retorted sharply that Davison was too partial and that she did not feel she could altogether trust him. Davison in desperation begged "to be allowed to retire from her service, and spend his days in prayer for her, as one whom salvation itself was not able to save if she continued the course she was in." (This account of the conversation appears in a letter from Davison to Leicester.)[41]

Davison, a seasoned diplomat with years of experience in bending to the Queen's pleasure, was dismayed by her reaction, but he cannot have been really surprised. However his employee William Brewster, a young man of very little experience in the ways of the Court, must have been profoundly shocked to discover how dangerous the service of the Queen could be.

The most influential of all the Queen's Councillors, Lord Burghley, the Lord Treasurer, who often opposed Leicester, supported him this time. Even before Davison's return to England, Burghley had written to Leicester of her Majesty's "discontent" about the acceptance of the title. For his own part, Burghley added, he considered Leicester's action "both honourable and profitable." He hoped that the passage of a little time would help.

During the early days of the Queen's displeasure, Burghley was recovering from a fall at his country home. Later he was felled by gout. Finally he limped back to Court and told the Queen that the results of the sort of rebuff to the Dutch that she planned would be so disastrous that he would offer his resignation if she kept to this course.

Gradually the matter began to assume more reasonable proportions. Sir Thomas Heneage was dispatched carrying a sharp letter of reprimand for Leicester from

Elizabeth. It began, "How contemptuously we conceive ourself to have been used by you, you shall by this bearer understand, whom we have expressly sent unto you to charge you withal."

However Heneage was given some latitude in his dealing with the Dutch and in instructions to Leicester.

Letters went back and forth across the English channel. Abject letters from Leicester somewhat mollified the Queen. So did a personal report to the Queen from one of Leicester's emissaries, Sir Thomas Sherley. During a walk in the garden with the Queen, Sherley told her that Leicester was seriously ill. He was suffering from a relapse of a disease for which a physician named Goodrowse had previously treated him. Perhaps the doctor could be sent to attend him in the Netherlands? The Queen was always concerned when illness threatened one of her circle and she quickly agreed to send Doctor Goodrowse. Sherley wrote to Leicester, "It moved her much and she answered me, that with all her heart you should have him, and that she was sorry that your lordship had that need of him."[42]

While Davison in London was attempting to present Leicester's actions in the most favorable light, Leicester in the Netherlands was complaining that Davison was not trying hard enough. In fact, he claimed peevishly, Davison had urged him to accept the post of Supreme Governor-General.

Leicester's letter of March 10, 1586, to Davison still exists. In the margin, the exasperated Davison jotted down comments refuting the charges. "Denied," he wrote firmly in the margin, or, "The contrary doth appear."

Leicester wrote, "It hath not grieved me a little that by your means I have fallen into her Majesty's so deep displeasure, but that you have so carelessly discharged your part in the due declaration of all things as they stood in truth." Davison, he said, had advised him to accept the Dutch offer: "Therefore I conclude, charging you with your conscience how you do deal now with me, seeing you chiefly brought me into it." Davison wrote in the margin: "Absolutely denied."

Continued Leicester, "I did very unwillingly come to the matter." Davison wrote, "Hereof let the world judge."

Finally, Leicester said petulantly, "Except your embassages have better success, I shall have no great cause to commend them."[43]

Davison knew how perilous life was for those close to the throne. Brewster was making this discovery as he watched his employer rise and fall in royal favor.

Incidentally, matters were not helped by a report, possibly true, that Lettice, Leicester's wife, was planning to join him in the Netherlands "with such a train of ladies and gentlewomen and such rich coaches, litters and side saddles as her Majesty had none such."[44]

The Queen greeted this news with "great oaths" and said she would have "no more courts under her obeisance than her own."[45] Lady Leicester stayed home.

Sir Philip Sidney in Flushing wrote to Davison the kind of letter calculated to smooth over the difference between Davison and Leicester: "Well Cousin, these mistakings sometimes breed hard effects, but I know he [Leicester] in his judgment loves you very well, howsoever in his passion he have written, and so I end, assuring you that I am still one toward you, as one that know you, and therefore love you."[46] Sidney was Leicester's nephew.

The campaign in the Netherlands dragged on, strictly

a defensive operation, as the Queen wanted it. She was engaged in secret peace negotiations with the Spanish. The Earl of Leicester came back to England in November 1586, remaining until the following July, when he went back to the Low Countries. He returned to England finally in November 1587.

In the shipyards of Spain, King Philip's men were building the Armada which was to sail against England and bring an end to the long half-war between Spain and England.

In the spring of 1586 Davison spent some time at his country home in Stepney, then returned to the Court. Perhaps Brewster took advantage of the lull to pay a visit to his own home in Scrooby, where he could recount his adventures in both London and the Low Countries.

Despite the Queen's anger at Davison over the Leicester appointment, she considered that, on balance, he had given her good service in the Netherlands and throughout his career. She named him a member of the Privy Council, the group of never more than twenty high officials who advised the Queen and carried out the country's business in her name. All were appointed personally by the Queen.[47]

On September 30, 1586, the Queen appointed Davison a principal Secretary of State. In this new post he worked closely with Sir Francis Walsingham, who was often ill then, and during these illnesses he substituted for Walsingham.

As any bureaucrat well knows, Davison's promotion was in effect a promotion for Brewster as well. The staff of a man "on the way up" receives prompt attention and invariably courteous treatment. It was also a position from which Brewster might follow the innermost workings of the Court and even hope for a successful career of his own.

Queen Elizabeth told the young Earl of Essex later that she had personally selected Davison for the situation, and she appeared to take credit for her discernment in appreciating his capability.[48]

Essex had returned a hero from the Netherlands. Not only had he performed well in the tournaments with which the young officers passed their time during lulls in the long, sluggish campaign, but he had fought bravely during the brief but furious battle at Zutphen.

While Davison and Brewster were still in the Netherlands, and later during the Leicester controversy, other events that were to end the services of both the Secretary and his clerk had begun to build.

Davison was only partially aware of the increasing threats to the life of Queen Elizabeth. She had lived with the danger a long time, carrying on in spite of it with her constant round of public progresses—trips to various parts of her kingdom—public appearances in London, and the almost totally public life of a Court where many people thronged about the sovereign.

It was an age of assassination: Henry Darnley, husband of Mary Queen of Scots, in 1567; the Earl of Murray, Regent for the infant King of Scotland, in 1570; Gaspard de Coligny, Admiral of France, in 1572; and William of Orange, in 1584. Before the decade was out, assassins would kill the Duke de Guise in the bedchamber of Henry III of France, and within months Henry himself would be stabbed by another assassin bent on avenging the Duke's death.

Plots against Elizabeth's life invariably involved the

hope for succession to the English throne of Mary Queen of Scots, who since 1568 had been in England, first as a refugee from the Scots and then as a prisoner. As a prisoner, Mary could do little more than offer encouragement to any efforts which might bring her freedom and perhaps the throne.

She offered encouragement to such efforts over the years, sending letters which were smuggled by her servants to the French ambassador in London, who then forwarded them by diplomatic pouch to Mary's agent in Paris or to others with whom she corresponded.

During most of her captivity in England, Mary was under the loosest kind of surveillance, permitted almost every freedom except the freedom to travel where she wished. She went riding and hunting under escort, journeyed occasionally to the baths at Buxton, maintained her own establishment of secretaries and ladies in waiting.

She and her establishment were moved from one country place to another as frequently as was required to escape the odors caused by the lack of sanitation of the time. After a period of "sweetening," the house would be habitable again, and the retinue could return.

In January 1585 Mary's household was moved to Tutbury Castle, a cold, drafty place she detested. She hated her new jailer too, Sir Amyas Paulet, who became her custodian in April. Much of her captivity had been passed in custody of the Earl of Shrewsbury, who treated her more like a guest than a prisoner.

Sir Amyas ordered the removal of the cloth of state, the royal symbol that hung above Mary's chair. It was a gratuitous insult and a token of the harsher treatment she could expect.

More important, Sir Amyas on instructions from Secretary Walsingham stopped the covert correspondence with the outside world which Mary had been conducting. She was still permitted to send letters to the French ambassador in London, but all letters were opened and read, either by Sir Amyas Paulet or by Secretary Walsingham. Mary knew this—it was not concealed from her—and she was frantic to re-establish a channel for uncensored correspondence. The French ambassador kept most of the letters sent through him to her from abroad until such a channel could be devised.[49]

In December 1585, about the time Davison and Brewster were witnessing Leicester's glorious reception in the Netherlands, a young Englishman named Gilbert Gifford returned to England from the continent. He had some training for the Roman Catholic priesthood in Rome, and more recently he had been in Paris, where he was in touch with Mary's agent, Thomas Morgan. When Gifford sailed for England, he had the mission of trying to re-establish secret correspondence with Mary. On landing, he was arrested by Walsingham's agents, and eventually brought before Walsingham himself.[50]

Walsingham, whose espionage network had long concentrated on the plots centered around Mary, took advantage of the opportunity Gifford's arrest presented. Gifford was recruited for counter-espionage as an English agent and was sent off to the French ambassador to volunteer to deliver to Mary the letters for her from abroad which had been piling up for a year or so.[51]

On December 24 Mary was moved from Tutbury to the Earl of Essex's manor house, Chartley Hall in Staffordshire, with Sir Amyas Paulet still her custodian. The security was intense. Chartley adjoined the property of the father of the spy Gilbert Gifford, and thus the plot and the plot to detect the plot moved forward together.

With Walsingham's knowledge and guidance, Gifford
set up a channel by which Mary could both receive and
send letters, which were intercepted and copied by Walsingham's agents. The letters were concealed in a waterproof package in the beer barrels sent to Mary's household from the local brewer, whom Gifford bribed.

As soon as the French ambassador in London gave letters destined for Mary to Gifford, Gifford turned them
over to Walsingham. The letters were in code, but the
code itself was one of the early deliveries, so this presented little problem. An employee of Walsingham,
Thomas Phelippes, an expert linguist, copied and de-
ciphered the letters. The original letters were then sent
to Paulet at Chartley. Paulet handed them back to Gifford, who gave them to the brewer. At that point the
brewer, who was accepting bribes from both sides, gave
the letters back to Paulet, who verified that the packet
was the same he had seen earlier. Only then were the
letters in their waterproof package ready to be inserted
in the bung hole of the keg and delivered to Mary.

The outgoing correspondence was handled similarly.
Mary dictated letters in French to her Secretary Claude
Nau. Another Secretary, Gilbert Curle, translated the letters into English. They were wrapped in their leather
packet for transmission in the empty keg. The brewer
handed the packet of letters to Gifford, who handed it
to Phelippes to decode and Walsingham to read. Gifford
then took the originals to the French embassy.[52]

Only six people were aware of the workings of the
secret post: Walsingham, Gifford, the brewer, Sir Amyas
Paulet, Phelippes, and the Queen of England. The brewer and Gifford knew only as much as they needed to be
told to play their roles.

In the late spring of 1586, this post was carrying the

first chapters of what came to be known as the Babington plot. Anthony Babington was a young, wealthy Catholic who had once been a page in the household of the Earl of Shrewsbury while Mary was in Shrewsbury's custody. As the plot developed, reflected in the clandestine correspondence, six friends of Babington were to assassinate Queen Elizabeth. Burghley, Walsingham, Hunsdon and Sir Francis Knollys were also to be slain. Meanwhile Babington himself and a few others would rescue Mary from Chartley, while Spanish troops coming from the Low Countries would invade England and English Catholics would rise in support of Mary.

Mary's letter of July 17, 1586, assenting in principle to Babington's schemes, was the letter that condemned her. Phelippes decoded the letter and sketched a gallows mark on the outside of it before giving it to Walsingham.[53]

From that point, events moved rapidly. One of the conspirators was arrested on August 4. On August 11, Mary was granted the unusual privilege of participating in a buck hunt, a pretense to assure her absence from Chartley. During the hunt, an emissary of Queen Elizabeth rode up to the hunting party and charged Mary with conspiring against Queen Elizabeth's life. Mary was taken to Tixall, another nearby house, while her papers at Chartley were seized. By September 20 Babington and six of the conspirators were executed in the peculiar combination of hanging and mutilation that the cruelty of the time devised. A day later seven more men were executed by hanging.

On October 11 the Privy Councillors and others named to try the Queen of Scots arrived for the trial at Fotheringhay Castle, where she had been moved. Acting in conformity with a statute passed by Parliament in 1585,

the commission to try Mary was to include 24 peers and
Privy Councillors. All the Privy Council members were
named to the commission.

Queen Elizabeth said that it was unnecessary to include
the most recently appointed Privy Councillors, Davison
and John Wooley, the Latin Secretary. Although they
were appointed to the commission, neither of them actually served on it.

The Queen and her Court were at Windsor. She rarely
went to Windsor, but during periods when she felt that
she was in especially great danger the castle's heavy
walls and layout made a secure command post.

With her was Davison, bearing heavier responsibility
than usual, since both Burghley and Walsingham were
serving on the trial commission. Fotheringhay, where
Mary's trial began, was about 75 miles from Windsor.
Brewster would have been with Davison.

While Burghley was still en route to Fotheringhay for
the trial, Davison wrote to him, in a letter intended for
Walsingham as well, "Your Lordships may, in my poor
judgment, but under your honourable correction, do a
necessary deed to persuade Her Majesty to be more cir-
cumspect of her person and spare to show herself publicly than she does, till the brunt of business now in
hand be well over blown; which I doubt not will prevail
more coming from your Lordship than for any other, for
the opinion she holdeth of you."[54]

Apparently Queen Elizabeth, despite her residence at
the more secure Windsor, was still not willing to isolate
herself as much as her advisors might have wished.

In England, the condemnation of Mary was almost
universal, by members of the Court and public alike. To
them, she represented a threat to the life of their own
beloved Queen and a threat of civil war. The threat would
end only with Mary's death.

Davison shared this view. He feared however that Elizabeth would be unwilling to take Mary's life "without extreme fear compel her."

Reports on the trial were hastily dispatched from Fotheringhay to the Queen and her principal secretary at Windsor. The night of October 15, after the long opening day of the trial, Burghley rode a few miles to his family estate, Burghley House, and wrote an account of it to Davison.

The Queen of Scots continued to protest her innocence. She demanded that proof of her guilt would have to rest in her own words or her own writing. The letters in evidence were of course encoded and in her secretary's writing.

With Burghley, Leicester and Walsingham all gone from the Court, Davison was Queen Elizabeth's principal confidant. She discussed with him what the reactions from France and Scotland might be if Mary were to be executed. She was afraid that James VI of Scotland, Mary's son, might serve as a rallying point for Elizabeth's foreign adversaries, leading to an invasion of England. James seemed always more interested in his own claim to succeed to the English throne than he was in his mother's claims, or indeed her life. But that could not be predicted with certainty.

After one such conversation with the Queen, Davison on October 29 wrote to Walsingham:

"The most material point she urged was the danger she stood in of the son, after the mother should be taken away, to whom all her [Mary's] friends would be ready to offer themselves. I let her see the fear to be utterly vain if she list to take such a course, as in honor and surety and good policy she ought, that her [Mary's] friends consisted of our enemies in religion, which could have no hope in him, remaining as he is." (James had

been reared as a Protestant. He had been a baby when his mother fled from Scotland.)

Davison continued, "Another scruple was that yet the King of Spain, having a title, might affect the kingdom for himself. The affecting of it I granted, but the likelihood of attaining it I impugned."[55]

Davison added, "This and a great deal more passed between her and me yesternight."

This was the peak of Davison's career, receiving the Queen's confidences and carrying on much of the work of the absent Councillors, as well as his own. It was the period when William Brewster learned the most about the responsibilities of high office, when the highest affairs of state were the day's business and after-hours rumors.

Despite the reassurances of Davison and others, the Queen was deeply troubled by the relentless course forward to Mary's execution.

Besides her fears of foreign reaction, Elizabeth was emotionally involved, personally, in this case as in no other during her reign. Mary was a crowned Queen, as was Elizabeth. There was something unthinkable about the execution of a death sentence on a Queen. Doubtless the prospect stirred Elizabeth's private childhood nightmares of the beheading of her own mother, Anne Boleyn, and of Catherine Howard, the fifth of the six wives of Henry VIII.

The strain on Elizabeth had been building during all of the years that Mary had been in England, with the growing realization that Mary's presence and the conspiracies centering around Mary spelled increasing danger to Elizabeth's life.

Elizabeth's behavior during the period before and after the trial was often irrational, sometimes hysterical.

Some time during the long night before Mary's trial began, Elizabeth summoned Davison and directed him "to write a few hasty and scribbled lines for stay of the sentence." Even before the trial began, its outcome was predictable.

Davison hoped that the letter would not arrive at Fotheringhay before the commissioners had reached a verdict. However it did, on the second day of the trial. The proceedings were immediately halted.[56]

Elizabeth set the next meeting of the commissioners for the Star Chamber in Westminster Hall in London. They convened there October 25, although Mary was not present. The commissioners questioned Mary's two secretaries, then unanimously found her guilty of participating in a conspiracy as "an imaginer and compasser of her Majesty's destruction."[57]

Parliament opened October 29 and promptly prepared a petition to Queen Elizabeth, requesting that the sentence of death called for by law be proclaimed. The Queen hesitated, urging Parliament to find "some other way to resolve the situation," presumably a sentence of life imprisonment in semi-solitary confinement which had been discussed. Parliament refused to change the sentence.

The first week in December Elizabeth permitted the death sentence to be proclaimed. Burghley and Walsingham drew up an order for Mary's execution, and on December 10 drafted orders for Sir Amyas Paulet at Fotheringhay to proceed to carry it out.

It was a strange, dreadful, waiting winter. The citizens of London rang bells and lit bonfires when the sentence was proclaimed and waited impatiently for it to be carried out as the days dragged by. The suspense was almost unbearable for the Queen, her Court, and the public.

The warrant needed only the Queen's signature, but the Queen hesitated.

She and her Court moved to Richmond Palace at the upper end of the tidal flow of the Thames. It was a favorite winter residence; near the end of her life she called the red-turreted palace "a warm winter box" to shelter her old age.

Davison was in the chambers assigned to him at Richmond early in December when he was summoned by Lord Burghley for a conference with him and Sir Francis Knollys. Burghley said that he had drawn up the execution warrant in obedience to the Queen's command. He told Davison to have it engrossed, then deliver it to the Queen.[58]

A few days later, Davison presented the engrossed warrant to the Queen. Elizabeth refused to sign it then, saying that the Spanish and French ambassadors were presently interceding with pleas that Mary's life be spared. She ordered him to keep the warrant, to be signed at "a more convenient time."[59]

The winter's gloom darkened with the mourning for Sir Philip Sidney. In the Netherlands in late September, Sidney, one of England's most popular nobles, was fatally wounded. His pregnant wife, Walsingham's daughter, was in the Netherlands with her husband and remained with him until his death on October 17. Sidney's own ship, the *Black Pinnace*, draped in black and with black sails, brought his body to a London in full mourning, arriving at Tower wharf on November 5.[60]

During a protracted period of mourning, it was considered a sin for any "gentleman of quality" to appear in any light or gaudy material.

Walsingham was burdened during this critical period

not only by his daughter's anguish, but by financial problems arising from Sidney's death. The funeral was delayed until February while Walsingham settled creditors' claims, which left Walsingham impoverished. He was often ill too, so that many of his government responsibilities fell to Davison.

By January a new plot against Queen Elizabeth's life was suspected, involving the French ambassador. The danger to Elizabeth appeared to be increasing, and the clamor for Mary's execution grew louder.

At last Lord Howard of Effingham, the Lord Admiral, a conservative Councillor whose father had been Elizabeth's great-uncle, met urgently with her at Greenwich Palace, the down-river palace to which she and her Court moved shortly before Christmas.

Lord Howard told her frankly that the public clamor for Mary's execution must be heeded, that the people felt that the continued delay endangered both the Queen and the country.

Reluctantly the Queen agreed. She ordered Lord Howard to have Davison bring the warrant for her signature. Davison, who was walking in the park which surrounded the palace, hurried in, conferred hastily with Lord Howard, and went to his room to pick up the warrant.[61]

This was the moment of decision for which all the Court had been waiting. There were other documents awaiting the Queen's signature. Davison placed the execution warrant among them.

The Queen received him "most graciously," according to Davison's later account.

Had he been out that fair morning? she asked. He really should have more exercise, it would be beneficial to his health.

And what did he have in his hand?

Different warrants and other things for her signature, Davison replied.

Had not the Lord Admiral ordered him to bring up the warrant for the execution of the Queen of Scots? Elizabeth demanded.

Yes, he had spoken with his Lordship and understood from him that it was her Majesty's pleasure that he should bring it to her for her signature.

The Queen asked for the warrant and read it through. She asked for a pen and ink, signed the warrant and laid it down. She told Davison that she had delayed because of her regard for her own reputation, that the world might perceive that however justly she felt provoked at Mary's offenses, yet that if any other means would have been devised for the security of her own person and of the state, she would have felt extremely sorry to have taken the course that now seemed necessary.

Then with a heavy irony, Elizabeth asked Davison, was he not heartily sorry to see the warrant signed?

He measured his reply: He was far from feeling pleasure in the misfortunes of anyone. Instead of wishing the death of the Scottish Queen, he could not be otherwise than sincerely grieved that a person of her rank and station, and one so nearly related to her Majesty, should render so fatal a resolution necessary. However, he added, as his sovereign's life was in danger so long as Mary lived, he thought every man must be of the opinion that her Majesty could not defer the execution without manifest injustice to herself and the whole realm. Consequently he could not feel sorry to see her adopt an honorable and just course for securing both. He preferred the death of the guilty rather than of the innocent.

The answer pleased the Queen. What else did he have

for her to sign? He presented some other papers and she signed them.

The Queen again referred to the death warrant. She ordered Davison to carry it immediately to the Great Seal as privately as possible. If the signing of the warrant were divulged before it was carried out, it might increase her danger, she said. He should "use dispatch" and send down the warrant to the commissioners at Fotheringhay with all possible expedition.

Furthermore, she absolutely forbade Davison to trouble her again on the subject or to let her hear any more about it until it was executed. She had now done all that law or justice could expect of her, she said.

She appointed the hall of Fotheringhay as the place for Mary's execution.

Davison told the Queen that he would take the warrant for the Seal immediately. No, the Queen said, he had some other business to transact; the warrant should wait until afternoon.

There was a further instruction. He should call on Secretary Walsingham, who was ill in his London house, to tell him that she had signed the warrant. "The grief he would feel on learning it would nearly kill him outright," the Queen said with a peculiar irony.

Davison picked up the papers.

It never should have been necessary for her to sign the warrant, the Queen complained. Sir Amyas Paulet could have saved her from the necessity. As if in an afterthought, she ordered Davison, with Walsingham, to write to Paulet and to Sir Drue Drury (who had joined Paulet in Mary's custody at Fotheringhay) "to sound their disposition as to privately dispatching the Queen of Scots."

Mary had often expressed the fear that she might be clandestinely put to death.

Davison's measured reply was that such a proposal would be merely labor lost, that he knew, from the wisdom and integrity of Drury and Paulet, that they would not, for any consideration, lend themselves to so unlawful an act.

He would, however, signify the Queen's pleasure to Mr. Secretary Walsingham. And so the strange interview ended.[62]

Davison immediately sought out Burghley. He found Leicester with him and told both of the developments. After dinner, he went to Walsingham's house. The news did not "kill him outright." Walsingham agreed in accordance with the Queen's instructions to draft the letter to Sir Amyas Paulet and Sir Drue Drury, in which the two custodians would be urged to assassinate their prisoner.

Davison took the warrant to the Lord Chancellor, and at about four or five o'clock in the afternoon, the Great Seal was affixed.

When Davison returned to Walsingham's house, the letter to Mary's custodians was ready. It expressed the Queen's wishes, quite bluntly: "She doth note in you both a lack of that care and zeal of her service that she looketh for at your hands, in that you have not, in all this time, of yourselves, without other provocation, found out some way to shorten the life of that Queen [Mary], considering the great peril she [Elizabeth] is subject unto hourly so long as the said Queen shall live."[63]

The letter would reach Fotheringhay the next day. Paulet was expected to burn it, but instead he kept it among his private papers.

Davison spent the night at his own house in London. In the morning an emissary of the Queen's directed him, if he had not already been to the Lord Chancellor for the

Great Seal, he should not do so until he had spoken again to her Majesty.

Davison hurried to the palace and was received by the Queen. Had the warrant passed the Seal? she asked him.

It had, he replied.

The answer did not please her. Why had he used such haste?

Davison answered that he had employed no more haste than her commands, his duty and hers required. In his opinion, he added, it was an affair not to be trifled with. Was it still her intention to proceed with the affair according to her former directions?

It was, she said, but she still thought the affair might have been done in a different manner. This way threw the whole weight on herself.

Davison replied that he did not know who else could bear the weight. It was clear that she still hoped Sir Amyas Paulet and Sir Drue Drury would have Mary killed.

The interview was disturbing to Davison, who talked over the situation with Lord Burghley and Sir Christopher Hatton and decided not to take any further action without support from other members of the Privy Council.[64]

The next day, February 3, the Privy Council convened in Burghley's chamber. Burghley had prepared a letter of instructions to the Earl of Shrewsbury and the Earl of Kent, the two officials who were to supervise Mary's execution. Each member of the Privy Council agreed that the warrant should be sent to Shrewsbury and Kent without again consulting the Queen. She had signed the warrant and commanded Davison not to let her hear any more of the affair until it was concluded, they reasoned.

The clerk of the Council, Robert Beale, was dispatched

to Fotheringhay with the warrant for Mary's execution
and with the letter of instructions, signed by the nine
members of the Privy Council who were present at the
meeting and by Walsingham, who signed it in his sick
bed at home. They all agreed with Lord Burghley that
the Queen had already done all that was necessary, and
they assumed responsibility for carrying out what they
believed to be her wishes. They would not reveal to her
that the warrant had been sent until it had been carried
out.[65]

After what must have been a restless night, Davison
again went to the Court on February 4. He found the
Queen conversing with Sir Walter Raleigh, her current
favorite. She interrupted that conversation and called to
Davison with the peculiar irony that characterized so
many of her remarks during this period. She had been
troubled during the night, she told him, by a dream that
the Queen of Scots had been executed. She had further
dreamed that she was "so greatly incensed against him
on learning of it, that in her passion she could have done
anything to him."

Davison was appalled. Again he asked if it was her final
intention to execute the sentence of the warrant.

"Yes," she said, with a vehement oath, but she thought
it might have been done in another way.

Again Davison explained his conviction that the way
provided by law was the best way.[66]

(That conversation may have taken place later than
February 4. Accounts disagree.)[67]

On Sunday, February 5, Davison carried to the Queen
the reply he had received from Sir Amyas Paulet and
Sir Drue Drury. They refused the suggestion to "privately dispatch" the Queen of Scots, thereby saving their
honor and probably their lives as well.

Paulet wrote plainly: "I am so unhappy to have lived to see this unhappy day in which I am required by direction from my most gracious sovereign to do an act which God and the law forbiddeth . . . My good livings and life are at her Majesty's disposition and I am ready to so lose them this next morrow, if it shall so please her, acknowledging that I hold them as of her mere and most gracious favour, and do not desire to enjoy them but with her Highness' good liking. But God forbid that I should make so foul a shipwreck of my conscience, or leave so great a blot to my poor posterity, to shed blood without law or warrant."[68]

Elizabeth was in a state of rage. She paced the gallery, muttering about the "niceness of those precise fellows" who showed great zeal in talking about their concern for her safety but who would do nothing to secure it.

The pressure on the Queen and those around her continued to mount daily. On Tuesday, February 7, Davison called on the Queen on some business unrelated to the execution. Again she brought up the danger in which she was living, saying that it was "more than time" that the affair was concluded. Again she swore a great oath and called it shameful in Davison and in the rest of the Council that they were careless of her safety and negligent of their own duty. Again she said that she had done all which the law required of her. She ordered him to write a sharp letter to Sir Amyas Paulet to hasten the warrant's execution.

Cautiously, Davison answered that the warrant, with her Majesty's signature and the Great Seal, would be quite sufficient. Send Paulet the letter anyway, she commanded. Sir Amyas "would look for it."

One of her ladies entered to ask the Queen's wishes about dinner, and so the interview ended.

It was the last time William Davison ever saw Queen Elizabeth.[69]

The following morning, Wednesday, February 8, Mary Queen of Scots was executed at Fotheringhay Castle.

Early that afternoon Lord Shrewsbury's oldest son, Lord Talbot, left Fotheringhay for the hard ride to London to break the news. He arrived at Greenwich Palace at about nine o'clock the next morning. Queen Elizabeth was going for a ride in the park surrounding the palace. No one dared tell her. It is still uncertain how she learned of Mary's death. The news travelled fast through the palace though, and spread throughout London, as the citizens of London once again lit bonfires and tolled bells. This may have been the first notice of it for Elizabeth.

Davison learned from Burghley that the sentence had been carried out and doubtless shared the nation's general relief that the suspense was ended. He returned to London for the night.

The next morning he arrived at Court to find several members of the Privy Council in Leicester's apartment. The Queen was furious with all of them, they told Davison, but above all with Davison. Sir Christopher Hatton described his own interview with the Queen after she learned of Mary's execution. She told him she had never commanded or intended the execution to be carried out; Davison had betrayed her trust by sending the warrant to Fotheringhay.[70]

The Councillors were accustomed to the storms of her Majesty's displeasure. Generally they eventually blew over, and it was wisest to stay away until they abated.

Davison went back to his London house, principally to avoid seeing the Queen, partly because he was not feeling well. He was suffering from palsy.

Saturday Elizabeth summoned her Council. Davison,

ill, remained at home. Secretary Wooley later wrote that she "rebuked us all exceedingly," which must surely be an understatement of the Queen's conduct when angry. She was angriest at Burghley of all those present, but she absolutely condemned the absent Davison. She commanded that he be imprisoned in the Tower, although the other members of the Council fell on their knees before her, pleading with her to take another course.[71]

In obedience to her commands, Lord Brockhurst went to Davison's house to take him to the Tower. He found that Davison was ill in bed and returned to Court for further instructions. Elizabeth, always sympathetic in case of illness, permitted a few days' delay, but on Tuesday, February 14, Lord Brockhurst escorted Davison to the Tower.[72]

How much did William Brewster know of Davison's role in the events leading up to the execution of the Queen of Scots? Probably, since Davison found Brewster "discreet and faithful" (as Bradford's history relates), he trusted him to know a great deal of it.

In any event Davison's tragedy soon became public knowledge.

Brewster remained in London, continuing on Davison's staff, hoping for his early release, and performing many services for him. Confinement in the Tower was sometimes relatively easy; prisoners were in some cases permitted to walk along the walks atop the broad walls, and to have visitors who brought books and other small comforts.

A few days after Davison was taken to the Tower, the funeral procession of Sir Philip Sidney finally marched up the slope, carrying his body to burial in St. Paul's Cathedral a short distance from the Tower. Marching in the procession of 700 mourners were the Earl of Leicester and the Earl of Essex. Sidney had left his sword to Essex.

When Burghley attempted to come to Davison's defense, the Queen ordered him to remain away from her presence and refused to receive letters from him. Burghley offered to resign all his appointments. In a draft of a letter probably never accepted by Elizabeth, Burghley wrote, "And having ended that concerning myself, I cannot in duty forebear to put your Majesty in mind that if Mr. Davison be committed to the Tower, who best knoweth his own cause, the example will be sorrowful to all your faithful servants and joyful to your enemies. And as I can remember many examples, in your father's, your brother's, your sister's, yea even your own time, of committing of Councillors either to other men's houses or to their own, so I can not remember any one example of a Councillor committed to the Tower, but where they are attainted afterwards of high treason; and so were served afterwards. And what your Majesty intendeth towards this your servant I know not; but sure I am, and I presume to have some judgment therein, I know not a man in the land so furnished universally for the place he had, neither know I any that can come near him."[73]

Davison had lost his place at Court and his freedom. He was in danger of also losing his life.

The Queen asked her judges "how far the law would touch Davison," with the implication that he might be tried for treason and put to death. Despite an early opinion from at least one judge that Elizabeth's prerogative was unlimited, that Davison could indeed be tried for treason, others advised her that under the law, Davison could be punished by fine and imprisonment but not by death.[74]

She even considered the possibility of sending Davison to Scotland for the Scots to punish. Many Scots were incensed by Mary's execution, and James VI was writing sharp denunciations, not so sharp that his own claim to the succession to the English throne was endangered. Finally Elizabeth decided against sending Davison to Scotland.[75]

Less than a week had passed between the time when Davison was a respected Council member, having daily interviews with the Queen at her palace, and the time when he was taken in disgrace to the Tower.

In the Tower he wrote an account for Walsingham of his actions in connection with the death warrant.

Following three preliminary questioning sessions in mid-March in his quarters at the Tower, Davison was brought for trial to the Court of the Star Chamber (named for its ceiling of painted stars) in Westminster Hall. The charges were misprision and contempt. The Court of the Star Chamber was used at that time to try cases which for one reason or another were deemed inappropriate for trial in the other royal courts. Star Chamber dealt with disobedience to royal commands. There was no jury, and the sessions were not public. Cases were usually tried before the Privy Council with the Chief Justices of the Queen's Bench and the Common Pleas.[76]

However, in Davison's case, none of the Privy Council members who had signed the instructions for Mary's execution were on the commission appointed by Elizabeth to try him. The commission included several peers, the Chief Justices, several other officials, and the Archbishops of Canterbury and York. The Archbishop of York was Edwin Sandys; Scrooby Manor was under his jurisdiction, and the Archbishop's patronage and that of other members of his family was helpful over the years to William Brewster's family.[77]

The trial began on March 28. Its verdict was determined from the outset. If the commission had found Davison to be innocent, it would by implication have found Queen Elizabeth responsible for the execution of Mary, and she had disclaimed responsibility.

Davison's defense was based primarily on his statement that the Queen had signed the warrant, saying, "Now you have it, let me be troubled no more with it."[78]

Further, he contended, would he not have been charged with negligence if an attack had been made on the Queen's life while he delayed in delivering the sealed and signed warrant?

One of the participants in the trial described the Secretary's appearance: "Davison, with a comely countenance, replenished with gravity, but a voice somewhat low (which he excused by late sickness)."

He was still suffering from palsy and his left arm was in a sling.

Davison kept silent in the Star Chamber about Elizabeth's suggestion that Mary be "privately dispatched" by Paulet and Drury. When the Queen's counsel pressed him with questions about his actions, he begged them, with tears running down his cheeks, not to "urge the matter any further." He would not contest against her Majesty, he said; she was his gracious sovereign and he her servant, and what she asserted he would not contradict.

Each of the commissioners delivered a separate opinion, but all concurred in the sentence of 10,000 marks fine and imprisonment in the Tower at the Queen's pleasure. Several of them noted extenuating circumstances. Archbishop Sandys said that he was "sorry for Mr. Davison, who did it neither wittingly nor willingly, as he thought, but of a good conscience, to cut off the common enemy." However, he added, "Neither honest or wise man in the world would have done as he did."

Lord Grey expressed the hope "that it might please the mighty God to put it into her Majesty's heart to remit him his punishment."

Davison was returned to the Tower, to remain as long as the Queen wished it.[79]

(William Camden, early 17th century historian, believed that Davison had been chosen as scapegoat from the first. He wrote: "Thus was Davison, a man of good ingenuity, but not well skilled in court arts, brought upon the court-stage of purpose [as most men thought] to act for a time this part in the tragedy; and soon after, the part being acted, and his stage attire laid aside, as if he had failed in the last act, he was thrust down from the stage, and not without the pity of many, shut up a long time in prison.")[80]

The Queen summoned Burghley to Court once to talk about the Netherlands, but railed at him about Mary's execution and sent him away again. Burghley was old now, and often ill, and he felt that his dedicated service had been ill repaid. Some time during this period of exile he wrote to a friend, "My chief sickness is grounded upon ingratitude, which is worse than a continual fever."[81]

The Queen agreed to receive Burghley's letters after a time, and finally ended the estrangement in late June by coming to visit at his home at Theobalds for several weeks.

Before that, though, he wrote to Leicester, "Why her Majesty useth me thus sharply, I know not. To some she

saith that she meant not that I should have gone from
the Court, to some she saith she may not admit me nor
give me an audience. I shall dispose myself to enjoy
God's favour and shall do nothing to deserve her dis-
favour. And if I be suffered to be a stranger to her affairs, I shall live a quiet life."[82]

The thought of a quiet life began to appeal also to
William Brewster. He remained in London for a time during Davison's imprisonment, doing what he could to help
him and hoping for his re-instatement. Davison continued to carry the title of Secretary.

The records of the Tower of London do not show
where Davison was imprisoned. Conditions for a prisoner
of his prominence were often surprisingly mild. A few
years later, during the reign of James I, Sir Walter
Raleigh though a prisoner was at one period dining every
night with the Keeper of the Tower and was experiment-
ing in a little chemist's laboratory in an attempt to make
medicines with herbs brought from America. He also
wrote his *History of the World* in the Tower. Raleigh's
fellow prisoner, the Irish scholar Florence, was writing a
history of Ireland, and still another, the Earl of Northumberland, was conferring with a group of mathemati-
cians who visited him almost daily in his imprisonment.[83]

Brewster probably was permitted to visit Davison in
the Tower and he performed various services for him.

Brewster might have found employment with some
other official if he had chosen to do so. George Cranmer,
the young man who was also a member of Davison's
staff, became secretary to Sir Henry Killegrew, then
ambassador to France. Eventually Cranmer went to Ireland as Lord Mountjoy's secretary and was fatally
wounded in battle there.

But William Brewster left the excitement, the vanity and the perils of life at Court behind him forever. He went home to Scrooby.

All his life he was sympathetic and compassionate toward those who were in misery, particularly toward those who had fallen from positions of high rank because of undeserved oppression. These, of all men, he said, should be pitied most.[84]

4 *The Making of a Rebel*

L IFE AT SCROOBY MANOR was both changed and unchanged. The quiet, broken at night only by the birds and little animals of the fens, was almost unnatural after the city sounds of London.

Over and over the drama of the last few months played itself out in William Brewster's memory: The rise to power of Davison, to the Privy Council itself, and those evenings when Davison returned to his quarters after his interviews with the glorious, all-powerful Queen of England; the suspense over the delay in the execution of Mary Queen of Scots; and finally Davison's disgrace, taken to the Tower like a traitor, falsely accused of betraying the Queen's orders.

There was still hope that his fortunes would change, and that he might be restored to the Queen's favor. His destiny was wholly in her hands; the decision lay in her whim. But Davison remained in prison and the Queen mentioned Mary's death only to wail that she had been betrayed by her Secretary.

Gradually the scenes at Court faded from Brewster's mind, and reality lay in the arrivals and dispatching of the post, entertaining the couriers when they changed horses and stopped for a bite to eat. William took on an increasing share of the responsibility for the postmaster's duties. He had arrived in Scrooby to find his father's health failing and Prudence Brewster doing much of the work.

The struggles for power and honors at the Court seemed far away, although from time to time the couriers of the post passed along the latest happenings.

There was little word of Davison, other than that he remained in prison. He was still referred to as Secretary Davison, a slim clue that he might be restored to favor.

In the spring and summer of 1588, nobody was talking about anything except the threatened Spanish invasion of England. It was common knowledge that the Spaniards were building an invasion fleet, and that Spanish soldiers in the Netherlands could quickly be ferried across the North Sea to storm the English coast.

A council of war was planning for the defense of the realm. One of its members was Sir John Norris, who commanded the English forces sent to the Netherlands at the time that Brewster accompanied Davison to deliver the Queen's pledge of help.

Couriers from London would have told Brewster about the first sightings of the Armada, on a July afternoon off Plymouth, and about the battle between Spanish and English ships silhouetted in the moonlight that night.

The couriers would have told him too about the spectacular visit to Tilbury of Queen Elizabeth to review her assembled troops who were charged with the defense of London. On a white horse she rode through the soldiers' lines to a piece of rising ground, where she dismounted and walked among the ranks. The soldiers vowed to defend her to the death when they heard her stirring words, which were written down and later read by many in distant parts of her kingdom.

The Queen told her soldiers that she came among them resolved "in the midst and heat of the battle, to live or die amongst you all, to lay down for my God, and for my kingdom, and for my people, my honour and my blood, even in the dust." And then she flung this challenge: "I know I have the body of a weak and feeble woman, but I have the heart and stomach of a king, and of a king of England too, and think foul scorn that Parma or Spain, or any prince of Europe should dare to invade the borders of my realm."[1]

The only Spaniards to reach the coasts of the British Isles were shipwrecked sailors washed ashore from the broken ships of the Invincible Armada. Superior English ships and seamanship, and finally severe storms, defeated the Armada and ended the Spanish threat to England.

Early in September the news from London was the death of the Earl of Leicester, still the Queen's favorite despite his vainglorious actions in the Netherlands. He died after a brief illness while on the way to the spa at Buxton, and she mourned him deeply.

After the defeat of the Armada, while the minds of the English were full of their victory, Secretary Davison was quietly released from prison in the fall of 1588 or a little later.[2] Davison went to his house in London, hoping for word from the Queen. His friends tried to intercede for his return to Court.

The Earl of Essex, a generous though impetuous man, tried to use his own rising place in the Queen's favor to persuade her to restore Davison to the Court. Essex wrote to Davison reporting that he "dared promise himself it would be done," hinting at the possibility for Davison of even "a better state." Essex told Davison, "She gave you many praises."[3]

However much the Queen enjoyed Essex's company, she was not influenced by him in affairs of state.

When Secretary Walsingham died in 1590, Davison's supporters, including Essex, tried to win for Davison the appointment as Walsingham's successor. Unbelievably, Essex even wrote to the son of Mary Stuart, James VI of Scotland, asking him to intercede with Elizabeth in Davison's behalf.

Davison made one last attempt of his own to regain favor. He wrote an abject letter to the Queen. A friend, Thomas Knevit, presented it to her, but she refused to accept it. Essex also attempted to give her the letter. Again she refused it.

All attempts were useless. Elizabeth told Essex with finality that he must "rest satisfied, for she was thus resolved."[4]

Walsingham's duties were given to Burghley and eventually to Burghley's son, Sir Robert Cecil, who served with distinction.

After this disappointment Davison left London forever to live in his house at Stepney. Although he never was permitted to return to the Court, he did not lose the life annuity of 100 pounds which had been granted by Elizabeth when she appointed him as Secretary. Apparently Davison either did not have to pay the fine or else it was remitted to him some time after he was released. This and other steps to save Davison from financial ruin were certainly taken with the Queen's covert approval. Sir Arthur Grey wrote to Davison that Davison was "in tolerably good favor with her" but that "in respect to her begun course, she might not, with honor saved, make show of it." And if she were to aid him privately, she said, "her Court was so fraught with lynxes' eyes that the motives of her doing so would be discovered."[5]

Davison, despite his fall from power, was able to do one last favor for William Brewster. He saved Brewster's new job for him.

While the health of William Brewster, Sr., was failing, his wife and young William took over many of the duties of the post. The father continued to do what he could; in June 1590, one of the members of a party accompanying the Earl of Worcester to Scotland on a diplomatic mission reported that the old man had furnished horses for them. The mission had the twin purposes of congratulating James VI of Scotland on his marriage to Princess Anne of Denmark and investing him with the insignia of the Order of the Garter.

When the Worcester party returned through Scrooby, they found that William Brewster, Sr., had died. Mrs. Brewster told them that young William had gone up to London "to sue for the place" as postmaster.[6]

He was almost too late.

Although William had been acting postmaster during much of his father's illness, he neglected to pursue his own permanent appointment as diligently as he should have. Shortly before the death of Brewster's father, the Controller of All Her Majesty's Posts Thomas Randolph also died. There had been an understanding with Randolph that young Brewster would succeed his father as postmaster. Walter H. Burgess, who wrote extensively about the Pilgrims (*The Pastor of the Pilgrims, a Biography of John Robinson*), said that the position of postmaster became a sort of family possession if the duties were faithfully attended to. He cited a similar family succession in the nearby Doncaster and Tuxford posts.[7]

However the new Master of the Posts, Sir John Stanhope, was not aware of his predecessor's arrangement about the Scrooby appointment, and young Brewster did not take the trouble to ask Stanhope to continue him in his post. Stanhope appointed his own cousin, Samuel Bevercotes, a lawyer of Gray's Inn, to be postmaster at Scrooby.

This stirred Brewster to action. He appealed to his former employer, William Davison, to use his good offices with Stanhope.

Although Brewster made the 150-mile journey from Scrooby to London and talked with a subordinate of Stanhope's—Thomas Mills, the paymaster of the posts—he apparently made no effort to apply directly to Stanhope. Stanhope was understandably annoyed by Brewster's aloofness, and embarrassed by his own promise of the job to a relative. However, he said the determining factor was whether or not William had actually ever been installed as Scrooby's postmaster, even before his father's death, as William claimed. Paymaster Mills bolstered William's claim; Mills told Stanhope that the late Comptroller had indeed accepted young Brewster "to exercise the place for defaults of his father's weakness."[8]

At this point Davison wrote to Stanhope on Brewster's behalf. The plea brought an irritated reply from Stanhope. "All this while, and to this hour," he wrote, "I never heard one word from young Brewster, he neither came to me, being in town, nor sent to me being absent, but as though I were to be overruled by others made his way according to his liking. I know my interest such as whether he had the place or no I can displace him, and think him worthily displaced for his contempt of me in not seeking me at all."[9]

Davison, reading this reply, realized that Brewster had at the least been tactless, but made another try at saving his job for him. Davison patiently jotted down the reasons "why young Brewster ought to be appointed" on the back of Stanhope's indignant letter to him. Presumably he put the notes into final form and sent them to Stanhope. Davison said that Brewster occupied the post long before his father's death, as indicated by the enrollment of his name on the rolls among the other posts, by his receipt of the fee for a year and a half, by the testimony of Paymaster Mills, who registered William's name and paid his wages, and by testimony of neighboring postmasters that he was performing the post duties.[10]

Stanhope was convinced. He agreed to continue Brewster's appointment, and Brewster served as postmaster until he was ready to leave Scrooby in 1607.

It was probably just as well that nobody during this controversy brought up the complaints of slow delivery of a dispatch sent from London to Berwick near the Scottish border in the summer of 1589, when William was presumably acting. On the Berwick-Newark stretch of road, which included Scrooby, that dispatch traveled at an average pace of less than two miles an hour, rather than the prescribed pace of seven miles an hour (five in winter). The postmaster was responsible for having at least two horses constantly ready to keep the mail moving.[11]

It was also just as well that nobody noticed that the grant of administration for the estate of William Brewster, Sr., said that his widow Prudence held the office of post when he died. Young William was administrator of the estate; his father had not made a will.[12]

Some time during the next few years, Prudence Brewster also died, and William married a girl named Mary. She was two years younger than he. Her last name is not known, although she may have been Mary Wentworth, daughter of Thomas Wentworth, who was bailiff-receiver at Scrooby Manor until his death in 1575, when the older William Brewster was named to succeed him. Wentworth did have a daughter named Mary. Walter H. Burgess, who had planned to write a biography of Brewster, thought that Mary Wentworth was probably Brewster's bride. (See note 12.) Mrs. Naomi D. Holloway of Boulder, Colo., has prepared a pedigree of Mary Wentworth tracing her ancestry back through a number of noble families and to King Edward I.

Genealogist John G. Hunt noted the clues pointing to Mary Wentworth[13] but later concluded that they were not convincing. In unpublished research which he generously shared with this writer, he suggests that William may have married Mary Wyrrall (sometimes spelled Worrall), daughter of another prominent local family. (Her pedigree, incidentally, also goes back to King Edward I.) Mr. Hunt cites the registered will dated 1600 of Sampson Mallorie (or Mallory), who left bequests to a nephew Edmund Worrall, and to two married nieces Elizabeth Savell and Marie Butho. The original will no longer exists but was copied long ago into the York register, with the likelihood of errors that copying always entails. (York Registry, vol. 28, fo. 207, 208; available in microfilm reproduced by the Church of Jesus Christ of Latter-day Saints.) Mr. Hunt suggests that Marie Worrall Butho was actually Mary Worrall Brewster. He believes that the copyist was writing from dictation, and that the person dictating distorted the name either because of carelessness or a speech defect. Mr. Hunt notes that he has not found the name "Butho" in any Yorkshire indices of the period, and that the will contains several other obvious errors (Morrall for Worrall in one instance; the phrase "I, the said Francis Mallorie" midway through the text of the will of Sampson Mallorie). Mr. Hunt adds that Mary Worrall (or Wyrrall) had an older half brother, Gervis, who was a first cousin of Mary Wentworth.

The Order of the Crown of Charlemagne in the United States of America at one point accepted Mary Wentworth as Mary Brewster. Mary Wentworth's ancestry is traced to the Emperor Charlemagne. However the Order's Genealogist General Timothy Field Beard, in *Pedigrees of Some of the Emperor Charlemagne's Descendants*, writes, "We have included the line in this book since the evidence is strong in the favor of the Wentworth line, but we are no longer accepting lineages through Mary Brewster for membership in The Order of the Crown of Charlemagne, as more English research in primary sources, such as chancery proceedings, must be done to prove this line beyond a doubt." (Aileen Lewers Langston and J. Orton Buck Jr., compilers, *Pedigrees of Some of the Emperor Charlemagne's Descendants*, Vol. II, Cottonport, La.: Order of the Crown of Charlemagne in the United States of America, 1974, pp. xcix-c.)

Nearly everything about Mary Brewster can only be inferred. She shared her husband's growing interest in religion; she shared his ability to adjust to radical changes. Her health was apparently good for many years; she lived through the dreadful first winter at Plymouth, and she survived the births of at least six children at a time when many women died in childbirth. She managed when William was in prison or hunted by the authorities. She must have been a capable, well-loved mother. All the children except one who died as a baby lived to become adults. The older children who remained in the Netherlands when the *Mayflower* sailed for America came over to join their parents as soon as they could. There are no indications of any family inharmony.

William and Mary Brewster's first son was born

August 12, 1593. They named him Jonathan, the name of
the courageous son of the Biblical King Saul and the loyal
friend of David. (Could this be a subtle tribute to Davison?) Jonathan was not a common Christian name in
England during that period, although parents often gave
their children Biblical names, especially after the Bible
became freely available in English translation in 1560.

(The birth date of Jonathan was later recorded in a
notebook kept by the Jonathan Brewster family; the first
pages were published in Vol. 1 of the *Mayflower Descendant*.)

The "Geneva" Bible, which was widely used and
which the Pilgrims carried to America, had been translated by English exiles in Geneva, Switzerland, during
the reign of Catholic Queen Mary. It was the first Bible
in English to divide the text into numbered verses.

For a long time, the Bible had been a forbidden book
as far as the ordinary Englishman was concerned. King
Henry VIII in 1530 issued a royal injunction forbidding
his subjects to buy or keep an English Bible. However,
five years later he permitted the issuance of Miles Cover-
dale's English version of the Bible. Laws passed in 1542
and 1543 made it illegal for servants, laborers and house-
wives to read it.[14] They probably didn't know how to
read anyway.

By 1571 Archbishop Whitgift sponsored a translation
known as the Bishop's Bible, and a copy was placed in
every cathedral. Edwin Sandys, Archbishop of York, was
one of the translators.

By the time James VI of Scotland settled into his
throne as James I of England, he ordered a revision of the
Bible, although not a fresh translation. He hoped it would
replace the popular Geneva Bible, which he hated. The

King James edition of the Bible, in the language of the generation which produced Shakespeare, Marlowe and Ben Jonson, has lived longer than any of James's other actions. It was issued in 1611.

By the time the King James edition was published, the Scrooby congregation had left England for the Netherlands. There and later in America they continued to use the Geneva Bible, probably partly to resist any of James's theological ideas, and partly because they were used to it. (In *Of Plymouth Plantation*, Bradford usually quotes from the Geneva Bible, but rarely from the King James version.)

It is hard—impossible—to recapture the exact emotions of that age on the subject of religion, but this was the motivation that sent Brewster and thousands of others into voluntary exile.

Of course exile was not in their minds in the beginning.

Men were still dying for their faith in the closing years of the 16th century. In 1593, the year that William and Mary Brewster's first child was born, Brewster's Cambridge classmate, John Penry, was executed. Brewster and Penry, a merry little Welshman, had enrolled at Peterhouse College the same day. A little more than a decade after his college days, Penry was being sought as the suspected writer of the "Martin Marprelate" tracts, a series of witty, biting pamphlets criticizing the practices of the Established Church and its clergy. Such material, in the opinion of the authorities, was calculated to incite rebellion. Penry was finally captured and sentenced to death. He had been associated with a Separatist Church in London. A few days before his execution, he sent its members a farewell message, urging them to prepare to go into exile abroad and to keep together. There was no hope that England would permit them to enjoy religious freedom, Penry wrote.

Two other men who had been at Cambridge in Brewster's time or a little earlier, John Greenwood and Henry Barrow, were hanged a few weeks before Penry's death. Their crime—sedition, notably publication of inflammatory pamphlets. John Udall, another Cambridge contemporary of Brewster's, died in prison in 1592. He too was suspected of writing the Marprelate tracts.

Most religious oppression during the early years of Elizabeth's reign was directed at Catholics, particularly at the missionary priests sent to England secretly from abroad. Most of them were Englishmen who had been educated on the continent for their mission. Later, however, Protestants who resisted the Established Church were hunted down too.

Early in Elizabeth's reign Parliament passed laws recognizing the Queen as the ultimate authority in ecclesiastical matters and prescribing the form of worship in the Established (Protestant) Church. The laws ordered the clergy not to administer and the laymen not to attend any other form of services. Church attendance was compulsory, under penalty of fine, but the fine was small and this provision of the law was rarely enforced. In actual practice, people had the choice of attending the Established Church or quietly attending none at all.

For those who attended the Established Church, there was an intellectual as well as spiritual hunger for good sermons, but it went generally unfulfilled outside of London. Queen Elizabeth thought it much safer for most preachers to read "homilies" to their congregations. Homilies were officially approved discourses, published in book form, and generally rather boring, especially on repetition. The number of homilies was limited, and when the preacher went through them once, he had to begin again. Certain preachers were licensed to preach; they could deliver their own original sermons. The others had to use the homilies.[15]

The Archbishop of York, Edwin Sandys, in a discourse before the Queen, pointed out that London was "reasonably furnished with good preachers" and that a few other cities had smaller numbers. However, he added, "People of the land otherwhere, especially in the north parts, pine away and perish for want of this saving food. They are much decayed for want of prophecy. Many there are that hear not a sermon for seven years, I might say seventeen."[16]

Good sermons were in great demand, not only by those who could come to hear them, but by those living at a distance. The words were sometimes taken down in a shorthand, transcribed, published in pamphlet form and sold. In printed form, they were passed from hand to hand, often for years.[17]

Thus a sermon Laurence Chaderton delivered at Cambridge in 1578 was reprinted by William Brewster about 40 years later in the Netherlands. Chaderton lashed out against the practices the Established Church was following, a recurrent theme of the Puritans. The church, Chaderton said, was "a huge mass of old and stinking works."[18]

The Queen regarded criticism of the church she headed as dangerous to her authority, and she stopped it when she could. She considered Puritanism "a sect of perilous consequence." Elizabeth ordered Archbishop Grindal to halt the practice of "prophesyings," discussions of theological points by the clergy to which lay church members were also admitted. Grindal defended the prophesyings as a means of educating the clergy. The Queen suspended him from his office as Archbishop. Archbishop Whitgift, who succeeded Grindal in 1583, was much more to the Queen's liking. He vigorously enforced conformity, not only in the church but in the grammar schools. The schoolmasters were licensed by the bishops or their subordinates.[19]

During the first few years that Brewster was postmaster at Scrooby, he continued to attend the Established Church, much as he missed the inspirational sermons to which he had become accustomed in London and Cambridge. He made several successful efforts to recruit good preachers for the churches of the countryside surrounding Scrooby.

The church of St. Wilfrid's across the road from Scrooby Manor still has a 16th century bench which is known as the Brewster pew. It is carved with the ancient Christian symbol of a running vine bearing grapes, and it may once have been part of a rood screen. Aside from the Brewster pew, there is nothing to connect William Brewster with St. Wilfrid's. Regular services may not have been held there during his time.

But he continued attending one of the Established Churches somewhere in the area on Sundays, and the rest of the week continued to perform the duties of postmaster, with the couriers a tenuous tie to the world beyond Scrooby. London and the Court seemed farther away than ever. In 1593, the year the Brewsters' first child was born, the Earl of Essex was taking his seat for the first time in the Privy Council. The Queen turned 60 years of age, and her subjects marvelled at her erect posture and formidable energy. An outbreak of plague was taking many lives in London. Playwright Christopher (Kit) Marlowe, a Cambridge contemporary of Brewster's, died that year in a brawl in a Deptford tavern. In

1595 Sir Walter Raleigh was sailing to Guiana in the New World to explore a land where fruits hung generously from the vines and trees and where there might be more gold than even the Spaniards had found in the Americas.

William Brewster lived his quiet life as it unfolded, "doing the best good he could and walking according to the light he saw, till the Lord revealed further unto him," as Bradford put it.[20] His neighbors liked and respected him.

In about 1600 the Brewsters' first daughter, Patience, was born. The date is an estimate; there is no record.

The next year, the couriers brought news that the Earl of Essex, once the Queen's favorite, had been beheaded in the courtyard of the Tower of London as the result of a wild ride through London with a small group of supporters. This escapade, the last of several Essex escapades, was generally regarded as a move against the Queen's authority. In a gesture reminiscent of Mary Queen of Scots he wore to his execution a scarlet waistcoat with scarlet sleeves.

In 1603 Queen Elizabeth herself died after a short illness, a sapphire ring Essex had given her still on her finger. Her cousin, Robert Carey, took the ring and rode up the Great North Road through Scrooby to Edinburgh, 397 miles in 60 hours. There he delivered the ring to James VI, Mary Stuart's son, who would henceforth be James I of England.

After Queen Elizabeth's funeral, the new monarch travelled down the Great North Road to claim his throne in London. From the road, his eye fell on Scrooby Manor as a likely hunting lodge, as Elizabeth's attention had been called twenty years or so earlier. The Manor was found to be in too great a state of disrepair for the King however, and the Brewsters were not disturbed.[21]

Neither were they disturbed in their increasing attendance at the sermons of Richard Clyfton, an experienced preacher with radical ideas about purifying the church. Clyfton had been preaching at the church at Babworth, six miles south of Scrooby, since 1586. His challenging sermons brought listeners from miles around and eventually brought increasing pressure on him from ecclesiastical authorities.

One Sunday morning in about 1602, Clyfton's congregation at Babworth included two young boys who hiked there from their homes at or near Austerfield, a little north of Scrooby.

One of the boys was 12-year-old William Bradford, attending the Babworth service at the urging of the other boy, who had been there before. Bradford's friend soon lost interest in the Sunday round-trip walks of 16 miles, but Bradford persisted. He had found something in the little country church that changed his life.

William Bradford's health as a young boy was poor, and he spent more time in reading and introspection than did other boys his age. He had been an orphan since his early childhood, and was in the care of his uncles, prosperous yeoman farmers who taught William to herd sheep and took him to the Established Church in Austerfield. Their relationship with the boy appears to have been one of duty but lacking in understanding. Bradford's recollection of the preacher, Clyfton, was of "a grave, fatherly old man," one key perhaps to Clyfton's strong attraction for Bradford.[22]

When William Bradford persisted in listening to the disturbing sermons at Babworth, his uncles angrily commanded him to stop this practice. It was corrupting the boy's mind, they felt, and it was dangerous to fly in the face of authority that had forbidden this kind of preaching. The neighbors scoffed at the boy. Cotton Mather wrote in his biographical sketch of Bradford, "Some lamented him; some derided him: All dissuaded him."[23]

The boy defied them all.

Long afterward, Bradford recalled Clyfton as "a grave and reverend preacher, who by his pains and diligence had done much good, and under God had been a means of the conversion of many." Bradford also remembered Clyfton's long, white beard.[24]

The sermons of another neighborhood preacher, John Smyth, in Gainsborough, eight miles east of Scrooby, also attracted the attention of both Bradford and the Brewsters. Both Clyfton and Smyth were graduates of that incubator of radical thought, Cambridge University. John Smyth brought his radical ideas about church government to Gainsborough in about 1602. It is not clear whether Smyth was a minister of the Established Church at Gainsborough; he may have merely acted in that capacity during the absence of a vicar.

At any rate, he soon attracted a following to his sermons, and he was "well beloved of most men," according to Bradford.

Bradford's uncles and his other relatives considered his trips to hear Smyth in Gainsborough even more objectionable than his visits to hear Clyfton in Babworth. They ordered him to stop them. Soon afterward some of the critical relations died suddenly. The survivors may have regarded this as a warning from heaven. They made no further strong objections, and the boy continued to listen to John Smyth's dissertations on his views of the true path for followers of God.[25]

Some time during these years William Brewster, then in his late thirties, met William Bradford, then in his early teens. They began a friendship characterized by absolute trust that lasted until Brewster's death in America some forty years later.

Most of what is known about Brewster comes from the Plymouth history that Bradford wrote. It is Bradford's most complete biography of any of the Pilgrims.

Bradford tells nothing of his friend's appearance; clearly this was never important to him. He thought of him always as "my dear and loving friend."

However Bradford did describe Brewster's character at length:

> "He was wise and discreet and well spoken, having a grave and deliberate utterance, of a very cheerful spirit, very sociable and pleasant amongst his friends, of a humble and modest mind, of a peaceable disposition, undervaluing himself and his own abilities and sometime overvaluing others. Inoffensive and innocent in his life and conversation, which gained him the love of those without as well as those within..."[26]

Brewster valued the friendship as much as Bradford did. In talks with young William Bradford, Brewster was perhaps reliving similar conversations twenty years earlier when Secretary Davison talked with him "as a friend and familiar." Now Brewster's own role was as a man of experience, probably as a father-figure for the orphaned Bradford during the first years of their acquaintance. Later, of course, they were equals.

William Bradford's formal education never went beyond the village school. (But then, neither did Shakespeare's!) Bradford nevertheless acquired a good liberal education, reading from the Bible and such books as John Foxe's *Actes & Monuments* (known as Foxe's Book of Martyrs, accounts of Protestants who had suffered for their faith during the reign of Queen Mary). He probably borrowed many books from Brewster, who may have served informally as his tutor.

Bradford's later knowledge of scripture was prodigious; he was always able to cite an appropriate Bible passage to illustrate a point. He knew some Latin and Greek, and toward the end of his life he was learning Hebrew, for his personal satisfaction in reading the scriptures.

The ideas expressed in the sermons of Smyth and Clyfton became the most important things in life to Brewster, Bradford and a little group of like-minded people. They were convinced that the elaborate ceremonies still practiced in the Established Church divided them from the proper worship of God, that they must restore its service to its "primitive order, liberty and beauty."[27] Since they could not reform the Established Church, they would separate from it. Similar convictions had stirred other groups in various parts of England to form their own separated churches; some of them had been suppressed, and some had fled to the greater religious toleration of Holland.

The Separatist movement had been growing for some time. During the 1593 session of Parliament Sir Walter Raleigh said that he believed, and was sorry for it, there might be ten or twelve thousand Brownists and their families in the Kingdom. The Separatists were often called Brownists because Robert Browne, a minister of the Established Church, had been an early leader of the movement. They disliked the name.

In 1606 or earlier, a small group formed a separated church in Gainsborough with John Smyth as minister and with the Brewsters and William Bradford as members of the congregation.

The Separatists believed that the only authority needed

to form a church was the desire of "two or three gathered together." They denied authority of the bishops, and this flouting of authority was considered a danger by both Established Church and State.

Within a short time, the Gainsborough group divided, apparently only because some of the members living farther away from the church found the distance too great. One group continued to meet at Gainsborough with John Smyth. The other group met at Scrooby and invited Richard Clyfton to be their minister. Clyfton's acceptance meant that the veteran preacher was leaving his post at Babworth and courageously casting his lot with the new illegally constituted church.

A few of the worshippers had been part of another Established Church at Worksop, west of Babworth. Its preacher was Richard Bernard, another Cambridge graduate, who wrote allegories similar to the works written later on by John Bunyan. With a hundred of his parishioners, Bernard briefly formed a separated congregation within the walls of his parish church. However in 1603 King James decreed that ministers of the Established Church were either to accept the prescribed ceremonies and other ecclesiastical restrictions or be discharged from their pulpits. About 300 English ministers lost their posts. Bernard drew back from following the Separatist course. Reconsidering his earlier views, he wrote, "Time is an instructor to a diligent searcher; I see now what then I saw not." He remained the vicar of Worksop.[28]

Although he did not follow Richard Clyfton of Babworth along the Separatist path, Bernard spoke of Clyfton as one whom he truly and entirely loved as a man devoted to God, and every way worthy of love for his irreprovable life and conversation. A portrait of Bernard —one of the very few portraits of those whose lives touched the Pilgrims—shows a stern, unsmiling man with searching eyes; he is wearing a tight-fitting black cap and a black clerical gown, with a white collar brushing up under his small beard.[29]

An important member of the new Scrooby group was John Robinson, about thirty years of age then, another Cambridge graduate. Robinson had been living in Sturton-le-Steeple, east of Scrooby, since he had been suspended from the exercise of his ministry at Norwich about 1604 under the King's order about non-conforming clergy. He joined the new Scrooby congregation, first as an ordinary member, although he had two Cambridge degrees and had been a fellow of Corpus Christi College. He became Clyfton's assistant, and shortly after the Pilgrims went to Holland, Robinson became their pastor.

Robinson was a wise leader and a true intellectual, as the books he wrote during the Holland stay show. They also show the development of a greater spirit of toleration and understanding than the leaders of the Plymouth colony in America often showed.

Except for William Bradford, John Robinson was probably closer to Brewster than any of the other members of the group. Robinson's wife, Bridget, and Mary Brewster were good friends too, and two of the Brewster children stayed with the Robinsons in Holland when the rest of the Brewster family sailed on the *Mayflower*.

The Scrooby church generally met at the Brewsters' home, its members quite aware of the irony that the Separatists who denied Episcopal authority were meeting in the bishop's Manor house. Bradford wrote dryly that "They ordinarily met at his house on the Lord's Day (which was a Manor of the bishop's)."

Brewster entertained them "with great love," Bradford said, adding that he made provision for them "to his great charge."[30] William Brewster was running the risk of the loss of his livelihood at the very least, and the further danger of imprisonment or death, and he knew it.

The news from London in November of 1605 told of a bizarre plot to blow up James I and Parliament on the opening day which James would attend. Searchers found barrels of gunpowder in the cellars of Parliament, stashed there by Guy Fawkes and a group of friends to avenge the persecution of Roman Catholics. Fawkes and the others were executed, and new measures were taken to weaken the Catholics.

Although the Catholics bore the brunt of religious oppression, non-conformist Protestants knew that the way they had chosen was also perilous.

Another daughter was born to the Brewsters in about 1606; the exact date is not known. They named her Fear. The Fear of God was their guiding star, and they feared men very little. They dismissed the early attempts to curb their meetings as "flea bitings."

Secrecy was impossible in the little village where anyone walking to the Manor on a Sunday morning or during any daylight hour could be plainly seen. Some of the neighbors looked on with increasing hostility, and local authorities began to act against the rebels. They imprisoned some for brief periods, and others escaped only because they were able to go into hiding with sympathetic friends in the countryside.

Clearly this condition could not continue. To leave their chosen spiritual path was unthinkable. Their only course was to go into exile, and the safest refuge lay in Holland, where they had heard that people could worship in freedom.

They considered the obstacles, but only to determine

how they might surmount them. English men and women could not legally leave England without royal permission. Very well, they would have to leave secretly and illegally, as there was no hope of obtaining permission.

The Dutch language was foreign to their ears (but not to Brewster's). True, but they would soon pick up enough words to meet their daily needs. Their main associations would be with their English friends in their own church and they would take their English Bibles with them.

Holland had been at war with Spain for nearly forty years. Was it wise to take their families into possible danger, even in the places secured by Dutch troops? Perhaps not, but no one could foretell the future, and peace negotiations were underway.

The Scrooby emigrants were, with few exceptions, farmers who knew how to earn a living at nothing else. Well, they could learn a trade as well as the next man. They could convert most of their goods into cash, as they surely could not carry much else with them, and with this little money they could live until they found new occupations in Holland.

They would be leaving their homes, relatives, friends; the green English countryside was all they had ever known. Still, their families and dearest friends would be going too. Their love for God as they knew him and for their church eclipsed all other considerations.

They were dauntless.

Early in 1607, the members of the Gainsborough church slipped away to Amsterdam, where they reformed under John Smyth's leadership.

The Scrooby congregation prepared to follow them. The Brewsters and the others made arrangements with friends who were remaining in England to take charge of property that could not be immediately sold or that might somehow be shipped to them later.

William Brewster left his job as postmaster, probably under pressure. In September 1607 the postmaster of Scrooby was a man named Francis Hall.[31] By this time the Brewsters and others may have already gone into hiding.

On September 15, William Blanchard, messenger (apparently an officer with the power to arrest), was ordered "to apprehend Richard Jackson and William Brewster of Scrooby, gentlemen, for Brownism, but he certifieth that he cannot find them nor understand where they are."[32]

In November Gervase Neville, a member of the Scrooby church, was summoned to appear before the Ecclesiastical Commission of the Province of York, which was charged with enforcing church conformity. Blanchard, the messenger, was apparently more successful in finding Neville and arresting him. Neville refused to take the oath or to answer the charges against him or to recognize the authority of the Archbishop. He was imprisoned in his Majesty's Castle of York, with an order "not permitting him to have any liberty or conference with any without special license." He was charged with membership in a sect of Barrowists or Brownists, with maintaining erroneous opinions and doctrine repugnant to the word of God.[33] (Separatists were sometimes called Barrowists, after Henry Barrow, another church reformer. Robert Browne returned to the Established Church after a period of rebellion; Barrow was executed in 1593.)

Despite the knowledge that emigration without a license to leave was forbidden, the Scrooby church members went forward with their plans to leave England. They were a body and they meant to leave together, although such a conspicuous exit was bound to be dangerous. They made arrangements with the master of a ship to charter his vessel for the trip to the Netherlands "wholly to themselves." The ship was to sail from River Haven near Boston in Lincolnshire on England's east coast.

The people from Scrooby somehow made their way the sixty or so miles to the coast, encumbered with their small children and the few goods they were able to carry with them to begin their new life.

The emigrants gathered at the place appointed for their rendezvous with the ship and looked out to sea in vain for a glimpse of sails. The sun went down, and the ship had not appeared. Finally at night, whether that same night or another one later on, the ship appeared.

With relief, the weary travelers climbed aboard ship, hoping that the often stormy North Sea would be fairly calm for their crossing. As soon as all the people and their belongings were on board, the treacherous captain of the ship called out to a group of English searchers who were waiting nearby in the darkness. The fugitives had been betrayed by the ship's master despite their payment of an exorbitant fee for their passage.

Roughly they were bundled into open boats, robbed of their money, books and any other possessions that tempted the officers. The officials searched the men to their shirts for money, and as Bradford recalled in his history "even the women further than became modesty."[34] As the dreadful night turned into day, they were taken to Boston and paraded through its streets to appear before the magistrates in the old Guildhall.

The magistrates sent a message to the Privy Council in London, reporting the arrests and asking for instructions. Meanwhile the prisoners were "committed to ward," in Bradford's phrase. He adds, "Indeed the magistrates used them courteously, and showed them what favour they could; but could not deliver them, till order came from the Council table."[35]

(Historian Roland G. Usher in *The Pilgrims and their History* suggests that the Scrooby refugees may have been detained in the homes of Boston families.)[36]

The authorities and townspeople of Boston included many sympathizers with the Puritan cause, and they were probably more lenient with the Pilgrims than those in many other parts of England would have been. Many Boston emigrants in the late 1620's settled the Massachusetts Bay colony and gave their city's name to Boston in the New World.

Instructions from the Privy Council finally came after a month. Seven of the principal men in the Scrooby party were to be kept in prison, to be tried at the next session of the Assizes (court). The others were dismissed and told to go back home, back to the homes they thought they had left forever.

Brewster, "the chief of those that were taken at Boston" (Bradford's words), was one of the seven who remained in confinement in Boston. He had suffered the greatest loss from the pilfering arresting officers. The seven may have been kept in cells on the ground floor of the Guildhall underneath the courtroom—stone cells about six feet by seven, each entered through an iron gate from the corridor.[37]

Mary Brewster was left to find her way back to Scrooby with teen-age Jonathan, seven-year-old Patience, and the baby, Fear, less than a year old. William Bradford was sent home too. They found shelter with friends or relatives and began to make plans for another attempt at escape. This was the first of the many trials and failures on the long, difficult road the Pilgrims were just beginning.

After a time the seven men detained at Boston were released; there is no record of any trial or sentence. By the standards of the time, Brewster and the others received extremely lenient treatment. Refusal to conform with the Established Church had brought long imprisonment to many in London, and deliberate acts of defiance had sometimes been punished by death.

In the case of the Scrooby people, it seems that the authorities tried to look the other way whenever possible.

In December 1607, possibly at the same time William Brewster was being held in Boston, or after his release, he was still being sought in Scrooby. The "wanted" records for December read, "William Brewster of Scrooby, gentleman. Information is given that he is a Brownist, and disobedient in matters of religion."[38]

Apparently Brewster could not be found, but a process was served against Richard Jackson of Scrooby, also disobedient in matters of religion. Jackson gave his word to appear before an ecclesiastical commission. However in the spring of 1608 the Archbishop of York sent the following notation to the Exchequer: "Richard Jackson, William Brewster and Robert Rochester, of Scrooby in the county of Nottingham, Brownists or Separatists; for a fine or amercement of 20 pounds apiece, set and imposed upon every one of them by Robert Abbot and Robert Snowdon, Doctors of Divinity, and Matthew Dodworth, Bachelor of Law, commissioners for causes ecclesiastical within the province of York, for not appearing before them upon lawful summons at the collegiate church of Southwell, 22nd day of April."[39]

By this time Brewster and his friends were already deep in plans for another attempt to escape from England. A few of the men visited ports and towns near the east coast and talked casually with the mariners, in hopes of finding a ship that would take them to Holland.

Finally at Hull they met a Dutch captain from the province of Zeeland, who had a ship of his own.

Cautiously they told him of their problems and of the disastrous earlier experience. The captain listened and agreed to take the party to the Netherlands. Have no fear, he told them, he would do well enough.[40]

The English hoped that the Dutch captain would be more faithful to his word than the English captain at Boston had been. They decided to trust him, and agreed on a secret rendezvous with the ship. Between Hull and Grimsby was an isolated common, well away from any town. The refugees were to gather there. The ship could anchor off shore and its passengers ferry out to it in row boats.

A bark, a small boat, had been obtained to carry the travelers' possessions from the Scrooby area to the coast. The women and children rode in the bark down the little streams that led to a river which opened into the North Sea. The men walked the forty or so miles to the rendezvous.

The bark carrying the women and children arrived a day early. One of the dreaded North Sea storms was already beginning to stir the coastal waters, and the women in the waiting bark were seasick. They begged the men in charge of their boat to moor it in one of the quiet creeks where they might rest over night and await the ship's arrival. By morning the Dutch ship arrived off shore at the rendezvous, but the tidal ebb had left the little bark grounded in the mud of the creek bottom. By noon it would be floated free by the rising tide, and there was nothing to do but wait to free it.

The men arrived from their 40-mile hike. The Dutch captain saw them walking about on shore, and sent a boat from the ship to bring the first load aboard, so that half the company could be loaded by the time the bark could be freed.

The first boatload of men climbed aboard the ship, and the rowboat started back to shore for another load. But as the boat started away from the ship, as the captain and his passengers watched the group still on shore, they saw a company of armed men descending on the refugees. Some of the searchers were on horseback, others were on foot. They carried guns and bills—long staffs terminating in hook-shaped blades—as well as other weapons.

"Sacremente!" the Dutch captain cursed. He feared that he, his sailors and his ship would be seized and at least detained by the English if he delayed. The wind was fair, and he determined to take his ship out of English waters at once. Hastily he ordered the sailors in the rowboat back on board, the anchor pulled up, and the sails hoisted.

As the armed pursuers swept down on the little knot of men on shore and the women and children in the mired bark, the ship put out to sea. In equal despair, the people on shore and the Scrooby men on the Dutch ship gazed across the waters between them as the ship's sails filled with wind and blew her on her voyage.

A few of the men still on shore managed to escape in the confusion, but William Brewster remained behind to be with his family, still on the bark, and to be of possible help to the women and children whose husbands and fathers were sailing away on the Dutch ship. The strength of his leadership helped the others face separation and their own capture.

The story of that voyage was not known by their frantic families for weeks. The men from the first boatload had only the clothing on their backs. Most of their money and other possessions were still on the bark. They were unable to help or even to share in the fate of the wives and children they had seen being taken away into captivity. Bradford wrote, "It drew tears from their eyes, and anything they had they would have given to have been ashore again."

The fair wind which had blown the first day soon turned into a fearful storm which drove the ship near the coast of Norway. For seven days they saw neither sun, moon nor stars, and even the mariners feared for their lives. In Bradford's words: "and once with shrieks and cries gave over all, as if the ship had been foundered in the sea and they sinking without recovery."

It is doubtful if any of the men from Scrooby had ever been at sea before, yet they were more dauntless than the sailors. The men from Scrooby firmly prayed, while the salty waters broke over the decks and drenched them, running into their mouths and ears.

"We sink! We sink!" the seamen were shouting as their distressed vessel pitched in the heavy seas.

"Yet Lord Thou canst save! Yet Lord Thou canst save!" their passengers shouted.

As they faithfully expected, the ship which had appeared in danger of foundering righted itself, and the mariners again were able to manage it. The storm began to abate.

At last, after 14 dreadful days at sea, the battered Dutch ship sailed into port in the Netherlands. Friends of the crew hurried to congratulate them on their deliverance from the long, severe storm which had been destructive to many other ships.

The English passengers gratefully walked on land again, found some way to send a message back home telling of their safe arrival, and waited with anxiety to learn what had happened on the English shore after the ship left it.

It was a pitiful little group of captives that the officers with their guns and bills had rounded up. They were herded off to the nearest town. Most of the women were crying because of their capture and because they were worried about their men aboard the Dutch ship or those who had escaped and were still being hunted down somewhere nearby. They shivered in the cold of the raw sea winds, and the children old enough to walk clung to their mothers' skirts in terror and stumbled along.

As before, they were brought before an officer of the court. The first justice before whom they appeared directed them to be taken to another, who seemed equally unsure what to do with them.

What, after all, were the charges? The poor women were simply trying to follow their husbands' directions, a sufficient argument in a 17th century English court. And what about the children? Could they all be sent back home and the troublesome problem solved in this way? There were no homes to go to. They had given up the homes.

The authorities apparently decided that the practical solution was to permit the refugees to leave the country, quietly, a few at a time. Some turned back, but most of them were still determined to leave. It took several months before the last of the emigrants were safely aboard an outgoing ship. Brewster was among the last to leave; he helped "the weakest" through the waiting period and secured passage for them. At last Brewster, Bradford and their white-bearded pastor, Richard Clyfton, were re-united with their friends in Amsterdam. It was August 1608.

Many years later William Bradford wrote the story of what he called "these first conflicts and sharp beginnings."[41] He concluded that the steadfast behavior of this little company and the news of their persecution inspired others to learn more about the Separatists' cause. Further, the knowledge of the troubles they had overcome in leaving England gave the exiles added courage for the trials which still lay ahead.

5 Refuge in the Lowlands

WILLIAM BREWSTER, finally re-united with his Scrooby neighbors in Amsterdam, walked along the city's prosperous streets and its busy canals with a sense of recognition and wonder.

This was the country where he had served under William Davison 23 years ago. Its landscape, architecture and speech were familiar to him. But much had changed. Although Dutch troops were still guarding their country, they were victorious Dutch troops and the fighting with Spain had ended in negotiations. The country was enjoying commercial prosperity, especially in its chief city of Amsterdam, which had grown in twenty years from 75,000 to 130,000.[1]

The Dutch Republic was the leading commercial country in Europe, or indeed of the world. Its ships carried goods to or from distant ports; the Dutch East India Company was paying dividends of from 20 to 50 percent.[2]

There was full employment, and work was regarded as an honorable way of life. This attitude struck a responsive chord with the English immigrants, who believed that a man's time should first be devoted to the worship of God and second to his work. In the England of James I and of Elizabeth, many members of the upper classes spent the greater part of their time in the pursuit of pleasure. This was not the case in the United Netherlands.

By the time Brewster arrived in Amsterdam, the early Scrooby arrivals had already found some kind of work and some kind of shelter, probably with the English Separatists who were already living in Amsterdam. For Brewster, Pastor Richard Clyfton and John Robinson, the highest priority was the nurture of their transplanted church.

The former Gainsborough pastor, John Smyth, was in charge of the congregation which had emigrated from Gainsborough in 1607. A group of Separatists from London, some of whom had settled in Amsterdam as early as 1595, formed another church, informally known as the Ancient Church. Bradford always referred to them as the Ancient Brethren.

To the dismay of Brewster, Robinson and Clyfton, both of these Amsterdam churches—Smyth's and the Ancient Brethren—appeared to be in danger of being torn to pieces by internal dissension, and the two churches were also disputing with each other.

This period was so painful for Bradford that in his history he glides over it with only a few lines about the Amsterdam stay.[3]

It would have seemed natural for the people from Scrooby to join once more with their neighbors from Gainsborough, the church of which they were formerly a part. They did not do so, primarily because of the bewildering behavior of the minister, John Smyth. Smyth, whose search for the truth had led him to separate from the Church of England, was still finding the truth illusive. He continued to pore over the scriptures and theological writings, reaching one temporary conclusion after another, sometimes rejecting a "truth" he had recently proclaimed. Thus, he determined that the English Bible was not truly the word of God, since it was but a translation and therefore only the word of men. The original Hebrew and Greek scriptures should be studied. Still, perhaps they too were not truly the word of God. No, that conclusion was too strong, but it would be better not to use the Bible in church services. Further, baptism, an act of faith, was necessary for a person to become a Christian, but most persons had been baptised as infants. Since this was done without their will, how could this be an act of faith? Smyth and his church "unchurched" themselves; Smyth baptised himself and then baptised the others. Eventually he announced the new discovery that his earlier conclusions had been a "damnable error."[4]

Much later, William Bradford charitably described Smyth as "a man of able gifts, and a good preacher, eminent in his time, but whose inconstancy, unstable judgment, and being suddenly carried away, soon overthrew him."[5]

This was the controversy into which the Scrooby emigrees stepped as soon as they stepped off the boats which carried them from England.

Their own minister, the white-bearded Richard Clyfton, disputed Smyth's contentions in writing in another of those theological controversies characteristic of the period.

Clearly the Scrooby members could not join with the faction-torn church led by Smyth, and they were not yet ready to reorganize as a separate church. Therefore, they worshipped with the Ancient Brethren, although they did not join that church. There they soon found troubles as unsettling as those in Smyth's church.

The Ancient Brethren—or to use their formal title, the Brethren of the Separation of the First English Church at Amsterdam—were a congregation of about 300. They were headed by Francis Johnson, who had been a fellow at Christ's College, Cambridge, during the period when Brewster was studying at Peterhouse College. In his Cambridge days, Johnson had been a tutor of John Smyth, now of the disputing Amsterdam church.

Johnson's credentials as a Puritan and a Separatist were impeccable. He had served a Separatist congregation in London with John Greenwood, and had been imprisoned along with other leaders for years. Then Johnson and three others were ordered exiled to North America and sent out with a group to found a colony for whale and walrus fishing on islands in the mouth of the St. Lawrence River. The expedition was a disaster. The French were already entrenched in those waters. After skirmishes with the French and Spanish Basque sailors, the ship carrying Johnson and his colleagues returned to England. In the confusion, Johnson and his friends escaped from England to Amsterdam, where they were subsequently joined by other refugees.[6]

Even during this earlier period, Francis Johnson was quarrelling with his brother George, also a Separatist, largely about the fashionable dress of Francis's wife. George thought it improper.

The brothers' quarrel continued in Amsterdam until George returned to England in the early 1600's. At that point, a newcomer, the Reverend Thomas White, arrived in Amsterdam with a group of Separatists from the west of England. Initially these people worshipped with the Ancient Brethren, then withdrew to found a church of their own, taking some of the Ancient Brethren with them. This drew fire from Johnson, which was countered

by a publication by White concerning "some of the errors
and abominations daily practiced and increased among
the English Company of the Separation." White charged,
among other things, that the Ancient Brethrens' elder,
Daniel Studley, was guilty of adultery and fornication
with women in the church. Studley and others mentioned
sued White for slander, but the Dutch court ruled in favor
of White. The court decided that he was telling the
truth.[7]

Despite this background, the Ancient Brethren were
still flourishing, with Francis Johnson as pastor and
Daniel Studley as elder, when the Pilgrims arrived. The
worship service appeared impressive to the newcomers;
years later Bradford wrote that the church contained
many worthy men and spoke of the "beauty and order"
of the worshippers.

Nevertheless Brewster and Robinson felt that the situation was dangerous for the stability of their own transplanted church and the peace of mind of the members.
They had left England at great sacrifice to establish
their own church, where the members might enjoy
mutual trust and love. They had not left England to join
in the controversy over either John Smyth's dizzying
theology or Daniel Studley's sexual sport.

Although they had arrived in Amsterdam only a few
months before, they decided to leave it.

Brewster's mind went back over the cities where he
and Davison had travelled in the early days of the English-Dutch alliance. How long ago it all seemed, when the
Earl of Leicester rode with his company in the king-like
splendor for which he always yearned, and when Davison
represented the Queen as her special agent, with his rising career and eventual disgrace still ahead of him.

In the winter of 1608, when Brewster was considering

the next move for the Scrooby church, Davison was dying in England. The registry of the church at Stepney,
England, Davison's country home, contains this burial
entry: "December 1608, William Davison, of Stepnie,
Esquire, sometyme secretary to Queen Elizabeth, xxiiij
day."[8]

The Pilgrims' minister, Richard Clyfton of the white
beard, decided to remain in Amsterdam with the Ancient
Brethren. From that point onward, John Robinson, who
had been the Scrooby church's "teacher," became its
pastor. Robinson, Brewster, Bradford, and some of the
others consulted on their next move. They decided on
Leyden.

At about that time, Johannes Polyander, a professor
at the University of Leyden, made this jesting assessment of his own situation:

> "Of the four quarters of the world, Europe is the
> noblest and nicest. The Low Countries are the best
> part of Europe. Of the seventeen provinces of the
> Low Countries, Holland is the richest, the most flour-
> ishing and the finest. The most beautiful and alto-
> gether charming city of Holland is Leyden. While
> the handsomest canal and the loveliest street in
> Leyden is the Rapenburg. Wherefore, I am lodged
> in the most beautiful spot in the world."[9]

More important to the Pilgrims than Leyden's beauty
was its reputation as a leading industrial city, where they
might find jobs. And most important of all was the prospect of peaceful life, untroubled by the problems of the
Amsterdam Separatists.

The Pilgrims needed the permission of the Dutch authorities at Leyden to move there. John Robinson made a
formal application to the Burgomasters and Court of Ley-

den, stating that about 100 English men and women wanted to come to the city to live "and to have the freedom thereof in carrying on their trades, without being a burden in the least to any one."[10]

The application was granted February 12, 1609, in a brief reply from the Court, declaring that "they refuse no honest persons free ingress to come and have their residence in this city, provided that such persons behave themselves, and submit to the laws and ordinances." Their coming, the Dutch authorities added, "will be agreeable and welcome."[11]

James I, continuing to take an interest in these Puritans he had harried out of England, ordered his ambassador to protest the Leyden officials' agreement to admit "certain Brownists," who, he inferred, were fugitives from English justice.[12]

Perhaps interference from an English sovereign would have been given more attention during the earlier period when the Dutch desperately needed English military assistance. However James had made England's peace with Spain in 1604. The Leyden authorities replied briefly that the decision to admit the newcomers had been made "without our having known, or yet knowing, that the petitioners had been banished from England, or belonged to the sect of the Brownists." A portrait of Jan Van Hout, Secretary of the City of Leyden, who drafted this reply, shows a man with grave eyes and a firm, judicious expression.[13]

While the Pilgrims were preparing to leave Amsterdam, the long Dutch-Spanish peace negotiations ended at last in a truce which both parties pledged to keep for twelve years. The truce signed April 9, 1609, acknowledged the liberty of the Netherlands after forty years of war. In celebration, bells rang in every city, artillery was fired and churches everywhere held services of thanksgiving.[14]

Within a few weeks after their application was granted, approximately 100 of the English men and women, with their children, left Amsterdam for Leyden. Once again, as in the departure from Scrooby, some remained behind, and some newcomers joined the group. The newcomers were either from John Smyth's troubled congregation or from the Ancient Brethren.

Brewster and Robinson had been prophetic in assessing the dangers of remaining with either group. John Smyth's church split, with the majority returning to London to establish one of the first Baptist churches. The remainder continued to meet as a small group for a few years but eventually, in the words of Bradford, "falling into some errours in the Low Countries, there (for the most part) buried themselves and their names." Smyth died in 1612. In his last published writing, he said that he was "ready still to change for the better."[15]

The disaster which struck the Ancient Brethren involved its fornicating elder, Daniel Studley, who was caught hiding behind a large basket in the bedroom of one of the women members. He was also accused of sexual misconduct with other women and of molesting little girls.

By 1610 the Ancient Brethren split, one part remaining with Francis Johnson and Studley, and the larger part under the leadership of Henry Ainsworth, whom the Pilgrims always regarded highly. They used his translation of the Psalms to sing in their services for many years. Ainsworth's little daughter had barely escaped from Studley, who was, he said, trying to ascertain the child's sex.

Richard Clyfton, the Scrooby group's original, white-bearded minister, remained with Johnson and even published a defense of Studley. Later realizing his error, he retracted the defense and finally broke off his association with Johnson and Studley. He died in Amsterdam in 1616 at the age of 63.

For a time Brewster and Robinson had tried to mediate between the quarrelling Amsterdam factions, but soon concluded that it was hopeless. What a relief it must have been to leave the wrangling behind them.

From this time forward, the church of the Pilgrims was generally a house of peace and harmony.

With the move to Leyden, William Brewster became the Ruling Elder of the church, an office he held until his death 34 years later. Bradford writes that Brewster was "called and chosen by the church," an early evidence of the growth of the democratic process in which the Pilgrims were to play a small, formative part.[16]

Robinson was the Preaching Elder or Pastor. At Scrooby, Clyfton had been Pastor, with Robinson as his assistant with the title of Teaching Elder or Teacher. Both of these were clerical officers, ordained by the ancient ceremony of "laying on of hands." Since Robinson was the only ordained minister of the Leyden congregation, the office of Teacher remained vacant.

Brewster was the principal lay leader of the church. He acted as Robinson's assistant in Leyden, and as the highest church officer during the early years in America. However he was never an ordained minister.

The second-ranking lay officer of the church at Leyden was Samuel Fuller, who had been one of the seceding Ancient Brethren from Amsterdam. In Holland, Fuller was a serge maker, but when the Pilgrims went to Plymouth, he was their physician and surgeon. His medical qualifications are unknown. The University of Leyden had a medical school; perhaps he had some connection with it. In any event the Pilgrims found his medical services satisfactory.

In Leyden once again the people from Scrooby found jobs and homes. They had known that Leyden, while a prosperous city, did not offer the economic opportunities available in Amsterdam. They considered that was a price they were willing to pay for tranquillity, and they made the best of it.

The English farmers learned the Dutch language and Dutch trades. Bradford became a fustian worker (fustian was a twilled fabric of cotton and linen). Leyden was the center of the profitable Dutch textile industries, whose greatest profit margin was in dyeing and dressing the manufactured cloth. William Brewster's son Jonathan, about 16 years old when they moved to Leyden, became a ribbon maker.

Other men became weavers, woolcombers, merchant tailors, wool carders, and so on. They worked from 12 to 15 hours a day and the pay was meager. They were inexperienced, and none were, at first, members of the Dutch craft guilds which controlled the skilled trades. The guilds required Dutch citizenship for their members; 33 from the English church became Dutch citizens during the next ten years.[17]

William Brewster never worked in the textile trades. He had greater financial resources originally than most of the others, and by careful management he and his family made them stretch. He also had his Cambridge education, with its grounding in Latin. The great glory of Leyden was the University of Leyden, regarded at that time as the leading university of Europe and superior to the

English universities. Students from many parts of Europe came to Leyden to study, among them some who wanted to learn the English language. Brewster used his knowledge of Latin grammar to set up an orderly system for teaching them English. Since everyone with any education knew Latin, it could serve as a bridge between any student's native language and English. Many of the students were Danes or Germans, drawn to the university, and some of them, Bradford said, were "great men's sons." The association with educated young men and the opportunity to use his own Latin skill brought Brewster much pleasure and enough money to meet his family's needs.[18]

During the first weeks in Leyden a child of the Brewsters died, probably a baby since the name is not recorded; infant mortality at the time was high. The register of St. Pancras church, Leyden, records the burial on Saturday, June 20, 1609, of a child of William Brewster. The age and sex of the child are not specified.[19]

A few days earlier, on June 12, Dutch records note that Ann Pecke, a minor, born at Launce, Notts. (probably Sutton-cum-Lound), and her guardian, William Brewster, had granted Thomas Simkinson, a merchant of Hull, power of attorney to receive on her behalf seven pounds sterling, presumably to forward to her. Ann Pecke had left the money with a Mr. Watkins, pastor of Claborough, before she departed from England. Ann and her brother Robert were both Brewster's wards, probably a niece and nephew. They lived with the family, perhaps contributing to the "great charge" which Bradford said that Brewster bore. Despite financial hardship, he was uncomplaining.[20]

The American genealogist John G. Hunt believes that

Thomas Simkinson, the merchant of Hull, was a son of John and Mary (Smythe) Simkinson. Mary Simkinson, a widow, married William Brewster, Sr, and became the mother of William of the *Mayflower*. Thus Thomas Simkinson was William's older half-brother. (The spelling of the name varies from Simkinson to Sinkinson to Symkinson.) The Pecke children were evidently the children of Robert and Prudence (Brewster) Pecke (or Peck). Prudence was apparently the daughter of William Brewster, Sr., by his second marriage—and hence was a younger half-sister of the *Mayflower* William. (See Hunt's article in *The American Genealogist*, Vol. 41, No. 1, 1965, p. 1.)[21]

On June 25, 1609, William and Mary Brewster, as well as Jonathan, appeared in a Dutch court as witnesses on behalf of an Amsterdam cloth merchant. The merchant had taken five pieces of cloth to the Brewsters' home with an eye to selling it to them. When the package was opened, one piece of cloth was found to be damaged. The merchant was suing the agent who supplied the cloth to him, and he needed the Brewsters' evidence. They confirmed the merchant's statements. The Dutch records list William Brewster, Englishman, aged about forty-two years; Mary Brewster, his wife, aged about forty years, and Jonathan Brewster, his son, aged about sixteen years.[22]

The records not only peg Brewster's age, they indicate that despite the hardships the Brewsters were at least able to buy an occasional piece of cloth.[23]

Consumer goods were readily available in the Netherlands at reasonable prices. Although the Pilgrims valued spiritual comfort far above secular things, they must have experienced many temporary frustrations because of the poverty. Bradford, paraphrasing a verse from Proverbs (24:34), writes of the early period, "For although they saw fair and beautiful cities, flowing with abundance of all sorts of wealth and riches, yet it was not long before they saw the grim and grisly face of poverty coming upon them like an armed man, with whom they must buckle and encounter, and from whom they could not fly.''[24]

However they were finally able to make a comfortable living for their families, at the price of hard labor and hours that were long even for that period. Despite the hardship, it was in many ways the most pleasant chapter in the Pilgrims' travels. Bradford says that they enjoyed "much sweet and delightful society and spiritual comfort together."[25] They had escaped from the persecution of the English king and church authorities. They had found homes and work in a beautiful city. Best of all, from their point of view, the church for which they had sacrificed so much was now firmly established under Robinson and Brewster, providing not only their Sabbath services but a focus for the life of their little community.

At first they held the services in the homes of various members. In 1611 the church members bought a large house to be used for church services and as a residence for Robinson's family. The house was located on the Kloksteeg, or Bell Alley, close to the cathedral church of St. Peter, nearly opposite the belfry in the rear of St. Peter's. The house is traditionally referred to as the house with the Green Gate, but this may have been originally a reference to its location, not its decoration. The deed describes "a house and ground with a garden situated on the west side thereof, standing and being in this city on the south side of the Pieter Kirckhoff [St. Peter's] near the belfry formerly called the Groene port [Green Gate]."[26]

The garden and ground ran back 125 feet. On the plot

of ground behind the house the English owners built 21 small dwellings, apparently for poorer members of the congregation.

A description of the service which meant so much to its members has no power to bring it to life now. There was an extemporaneous prayer by Pastor Robinson, a reading of two or three chapters of the Bible in English, with explanation of the passage by Brewster, the singing of psalms in English (Ainsworth's translations) without musical accompaniment, and a sermon lasting several hours in which Robinson explained the application of the scripture passage to the individual lives of his hearers or otherwise discussed points of doctrine. At stated intervals, Robinson administered the sacraments of communion or baptism. A collection to meet the needs of the church and of the poor was taken up. Following the service, Robinson and Brewster disposed of matters of discipline. Sometimes disputes between the members were decided in the open church meeting, sometimes privately in a session with Robinson. The church was a personal force in the lives of its members, who expected "correction" of their faults from the pastor or elder.[27]

This correction practice contributed to the destruction of the Ancient Brethren because of the abrasive character of their leaders. But with the church at Leyden, the personalities of Robinson and Brewster with their love of justice and their ability to guide without causing resentment drew the continued affection and respect of the members and served to strengthen the church.

Bradford said of Pastor Robinson, "It was hard to judge whether he delighted more in having such a people, or they in having such a pastor." The members of the church at Leyden, Bradford added, "came as near the primitive pattern of the first churches as any other church of these later times have done."[28]

Robinson was truly a remarkable man, cheerful and sympathetic, and gradually becoming more liberal toward people of other Christian churches. He wrote several books—essays on ethics and Christian behavior and on his own reasons for separating from the Church of England. His longest work was *A Justification of Separation from the Church of England, against Mr. Richard Bernard: his Invective.* It was addressed to his former neighboring clergyman in Worksop, Richard Bernard.

The members of the Leyden church were delighted when the Dutch invited Robinson to join a debate on matters of theology which was raging at Leyden University midway during the Pilgrims' stay in Leyden. Robinson enjoyed good relations with the Dutch church, the city government and the university. He matriculated in 1615 as a student in theology at Leyden University.[29]

In addition to the formal Sunday morning service, the Leyden church members met again Sunday afternoon for an exercise called "prophesying." Robinson or Brewster spoke briefly on a Bible passage, and men of the church joined in an informal discussion of the subject. Not the women—their role was to remain silent and on their own side of the aisle; the sexes were seated separately. The Pilgrims took very literally St. Paul's admonition that women were to remain silent in the church. There was also a service on Thursday evenings.[30]

William Brewster and his family lived in a house near the Robinsons on a street with the unattractive name of Stink Alley, the Stincksteeg.[31] Perhaps the name was a hangover from an unpleasant earlier period; at any rate the location seemed to satisfy the Brewsters. They named the baby born in 1611 "Love," probably reflecting the spiritual love of the members of their little community for God and for each other. In 1614, the last Brewster son, Wrestling, was born. His name indicates the obligation to wrestle with temptation. (The historian Samuel Eliot Morison points out that Bradford spelled the name Wrastle, and it must have been pronounced that way.)[32]

Bradford, who had been living with the Brewsters since they left England, moved to a house of his own. When he became 21 in 1611 he was able to claim and sell the property he had inherited in England—nine and one-half acres with a house, cottage, garden and orchard. He used some of the money to buy a house near the church and set up his own loom. In 1613 he was married.[33]

The bride was 16-year-old Dorothy May, daughter of Henry May, an elder of Amsterdam's Ancient Brethren. Bradford must have made frequent trips from Leyden to Amsterdam during the four years he had been living in Leyden and while Dorothy was growing up. The marriage took place in Amsterdam on December 10. It was a civil ceremony, since the Separatists believed that church weddings were not authorized by the Bible.[34]

There were lots of marriages in the Leyden days, lots of new households and many new babies. Forty-six marriages took place among the English while they were in Leyden, an indication that the church had grown from its original membership and that most of the members were young.[35]

The Dutch records list William Brewster as a witness for at least two betrothals: Mrs. Robinson's sister, Jane White, married a looking-glass maker from London, Randall Thickins, in 1612; Wybra Hanson married William Pontus, weaver of fustians, in 1610.[36] William and

Wybra Pontus finally joined their friends in Plymouth in 1633.

The Brewsters' oldest son, Jonathan, was married in 1615, but the name of his wife is unknown. She and her baby died four years later.[37]

It is still possible to see much of the Holland that the Pilgrims saw. Many of the buildings they walked past daily are still standing, although the Green Gate house is gone. Many of the scenes that have vanished were preserved by the great Dutch painters of the early and middle 17th century, who were recording for all time the sight of sailing ships in a Dutch harbor, of a couple dancing in their dooryard while their friends watched, of the civic guard, and of many other aspects of everyday life. Rembrandt van Rijn was born in Leyden in 1606 and was growing up there during the Pilgrims' Leyden stay. Frans Hals was forty years old when the Pilgrims left Holland, and his portraits of the Dutch people of Haarlem show the faces of people like those the Pilgrims must have known. In *Civilisation*, Kenneth Clark writes that because of the Dutch artists, "We know more about what the seventeenth-century Dutch looked like than we do about any other society, except perhaps the first-century Romans."[38]

The Pilgrims were to take to America many sweet memories of beautiful Leyden, its tree-bordered canals crossed by stone bridges, its stately houses rising above broad, brick-paved streets, and its industrious, tolerant people. They must have sometimes longed, during those first years in America, for the society they shared in Leyden, particularly after so many died during the first Plymouth winter. But not one of the Plymouth settlers ever returned to Leyden.

William Brewster's house, which fronted on the Stincksteeg, was L-shaped, and one door opened into an adjacent lane, the Koorsteeg. It is Choir Alley in English, and Vicus Chorali in Latin. Using Vicus Chorali as the address, Brewster began to publish books from an upper floor of his house in 1616 or 1617.[39]

His associate in the publishing business and his financial backer was an Englishman with the confusingly similar name of Brewer—Thomas Brewer. Thomas Brewer was probably never a member of the Separatist Church at Leyden. He may have been a member of the English-speaking branch of the Dutch Reformed Church, which was behind Robinson's house and with which the English Separatists always had friendly relations. At any rate he was of the Kentish gentry, about 36 years old when he and Brewster began their publishing business, and for several years he had been living in a large house called the Groenehuis, or Green House, a few doors away from John Robinson's house in Bell Alley. Thomas Brewer was studying literature at the University of Leyden. Several other university students also lived at his house, including Hugh Goodyear, an English theology scholar who was for many years minister of the English-speaking branch of the Dutch Reformed Church in Leyden.[40]

Thomas Brewer furnished the capital to purchase the type and other equipment used to print the books issued by the Choir Alley Press. They were certainly set in type in William Brewster's garret, but they may have been run off in one of the Dutch printing establishments.[41]

Probably the first book printed from Brewster's garret was a Dutch translation of Dod and Cleaver's *Tenne Commandements*. This book bears the legend that it was printed "Tot Leyden, Voor Guiliaem Brewster, Boeckdrucker, Anno. 1617."[42]

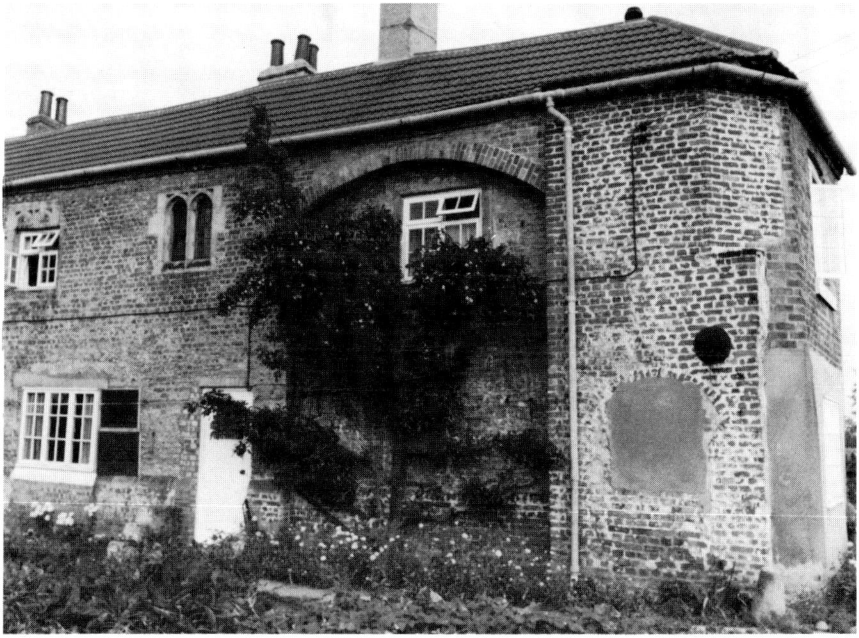

Robert B. Sherwood

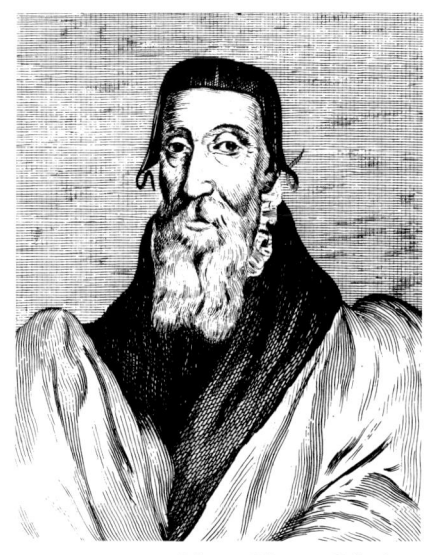

All that remains on the site of Scrooby Manor. The stone double-window arches in the second story appear older than other details, but the 12th century Manor house was mostly of timber.

As Archbishop of York, Edwin Sandys had jurisdiction over Scrooby Manor and would have stayed there whenever he had duties in that area. After the execution of Mary Queen of Scots, he served on the commission to try William Davison.

Library of Congress Collections

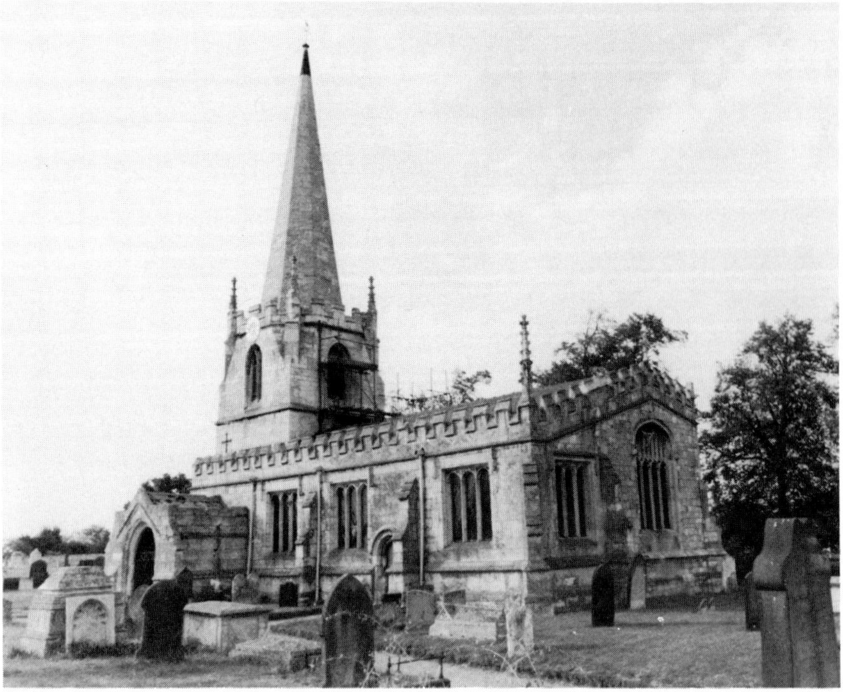

Robert B. Sherwood

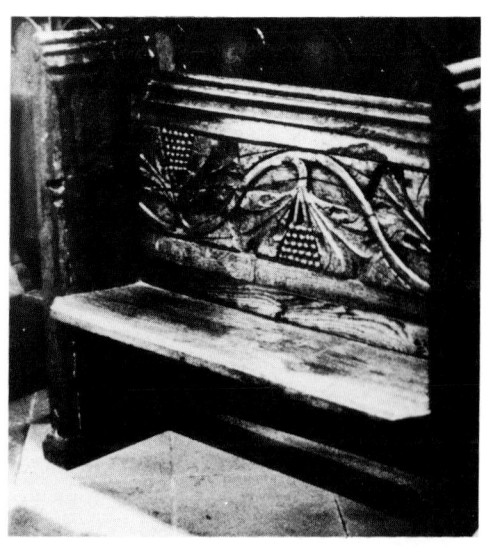

St. Wilfrid's church in the village of Scrooby. It stands across the old Great North Road from Scrooby Manor. The church was rebuilt in 1380, and the tower is of that period, although many later restorations were made.

A "Brewster pew," one of three similar benches at St. Wilfrid's church in Scrooby. Another is in Pilgrim Hall, Plymouth, Mass. They have long been known as the Brewster pews, but the origin is uncertain. The carving of the running vine is an ancient Christian symbol.

Robert B. Sherwood

Peterhouse College, Cambridge University.

Robert B. Sherwood

From the Registrar's record of students entering Peterhouse College, Cambridge University, on December 3, 1580. (Date at upper right.) William Brewster is the fourth name in the long column. John Penry is sixth.

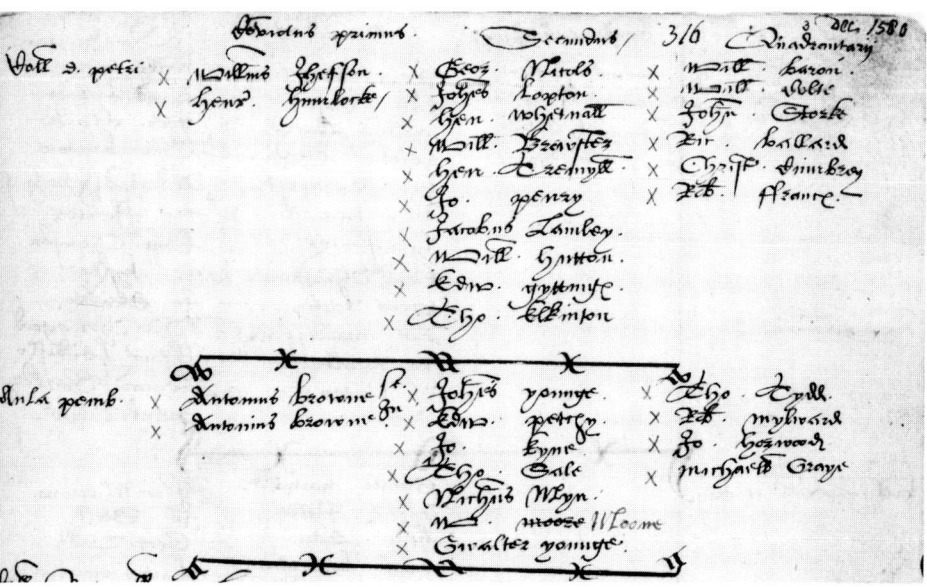

Secretary William Davison presenting the death warrant of Mary
Queen of Scots to Queen Elizabeth I. She signed it, but blamed
Davison for Mary's execution. (James Rogers Rice, Am., after
Julius Friedrich Anton Schrader, 1815–1900, Ger.)

Sketches from John Brown's 1895 book,
The Pilgrim Fathers of New England.

Cells where Brewster and others were detained after the
first attempt to escape to the Netherlands. They were taken
to the Boston, England, Guildhall (lower right), brought
before magistrates in its courtroom, then taken through
a trap door opening down winding stairs to the cells.

PERTH ASSEMBLY.

CONTAINING

1 The Proceedings thereof.
2 The Proofe of the Nullitie thereof.
3 Reasons presented thereto against the receiving the fiue new *Articles* imposed.
4 The oppositenesse of it to the proceedings and oath of the whole state of the Land. *An.*1581.
5 Proofes of the unlawfulnesse of the said fiue Articles, *viz.* 1. Kneeling in the act of Receiving the Lords Supper. 2. Holy daies. 3. Bishopping. 4. Private Baptisme. 5. Private Communion.

EXOD. 20. 7.

Thou shalt not take the name of the Lord thy God in vaine, for the Lord will not hold him guiltlesse that taketh his name in vaine.

COLOS. 2. 8.

Beware lest there be any that spoyle you through Philosophy & vain deceit, through the traditions of men, according to the rudiments of the World, and not of Christ.

MDCXIX.

The title page of the book that spelled the end of Brewster's Choir Alley Press and sent Brewster into hiding.

The Embarkation of the Pilgrims at Delft Haven, Holland, Robert W. Weir's huge painting in the U.S. Capitol rotunda.

William Brewster, center, holds a Bible. His portrait, like the other portraits, is imagined. Also in the rotunda, 58 feet above the floor, is a frescoed frieze. A panel depicting the Pilgrims' landing at Plymouth was painted by Constantino Brumidi.

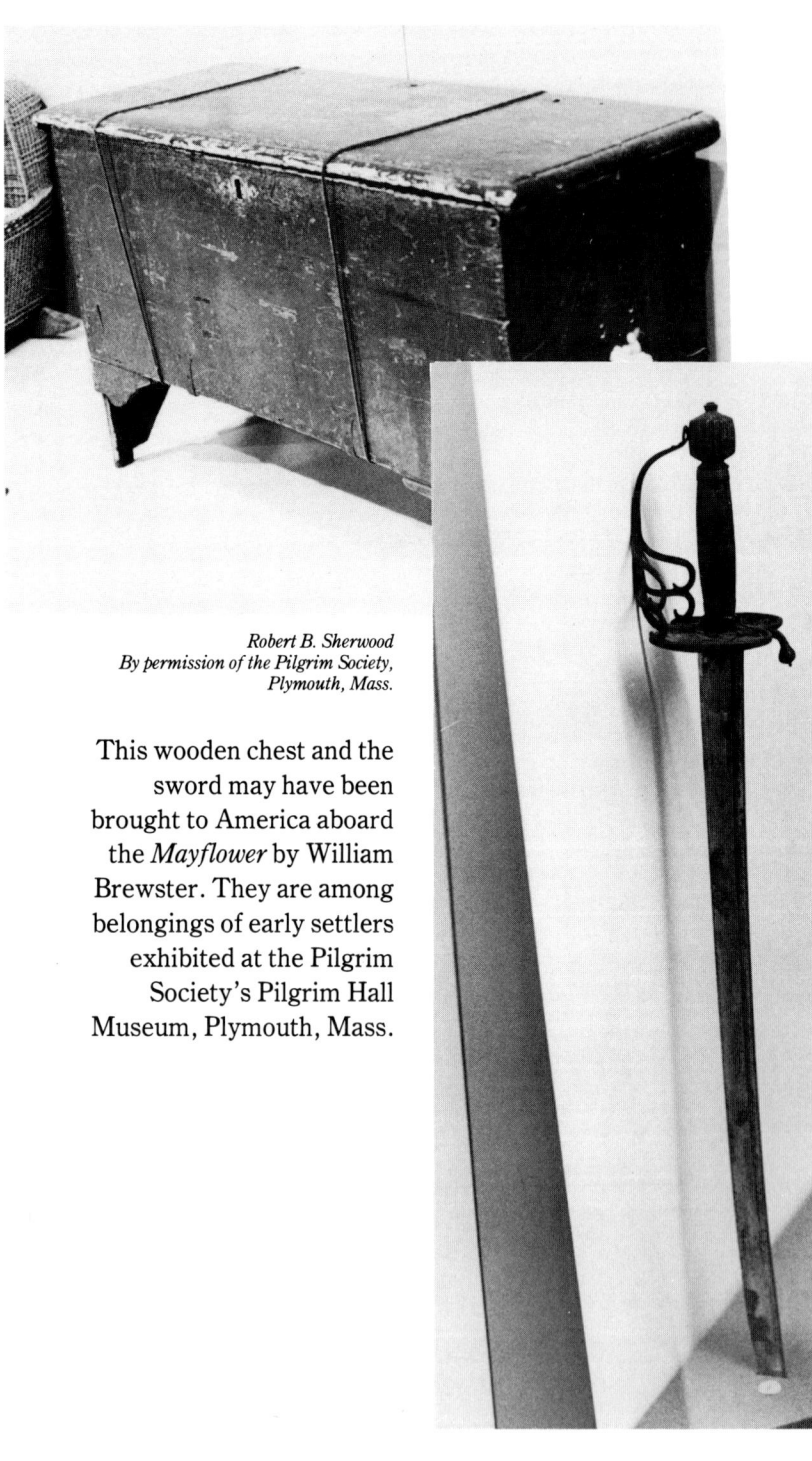

This wooden chest and the sword may have been brought to America aboard the *Mayflower* by William Brewster. They are among belongings of early settlers exhibited at the Pilgrim Society's Pilgrim Hall Museum, Plymouth, Mass.

William Brewster signing the Mayflower Compact. Allyn Cox made this sketch for the oil mural he painted in the early 1980's on a vaulted corridor ceiling in the House wing of the U.S. Capitol. Myles Standish stands at Brewster's right; others are unidentified. Cox is a descendant of Brewster.

Robert B. Sherwood
Courtesy of the Architect of the Capitol

Cliff Young painted this portrait of William Brewster for the U.S. Capitol in the early 1980's. It is in the center ceiling of a corridor in the House of Representatives wing, just above the Mayflower Compact signing.

Robert B. Sherwood
Courtesy of the Architect of the Capitol

Brewster and Standish in center portion of the oil mural of the Mayflower Compact signing, painted by Allyn Cox for the U.S. Capitol.

Library of Congress Collections

A 19th century artist's conception of how William Brewster may have looked. No portrait of him was ever painted from life.

Library of Congress Collections

Another 19th century artist's representation of Brewster. Like many others, it was inspired by Weir's "Embarkation" painting.

Captain John Smith's 1614 map of New England. He published it in his book about his travels, which the Pilgrims studied before leaving Holland. Cape Cod had been known as Cape Cod among mariners since 1602, although it appears on the map as Cape James in honor of James I.

A 20th century view toward Plymouth harbor from the hill where the combined Common House and Fort once stood.

Robert B. Sherwood

Courtesy of Plimoth Plantation

The Pilgrims' village of about 1627 has been re-created on another hillside a few miles from the original settlement. The village at Plimoth Plantation is open to visitors from April through November.

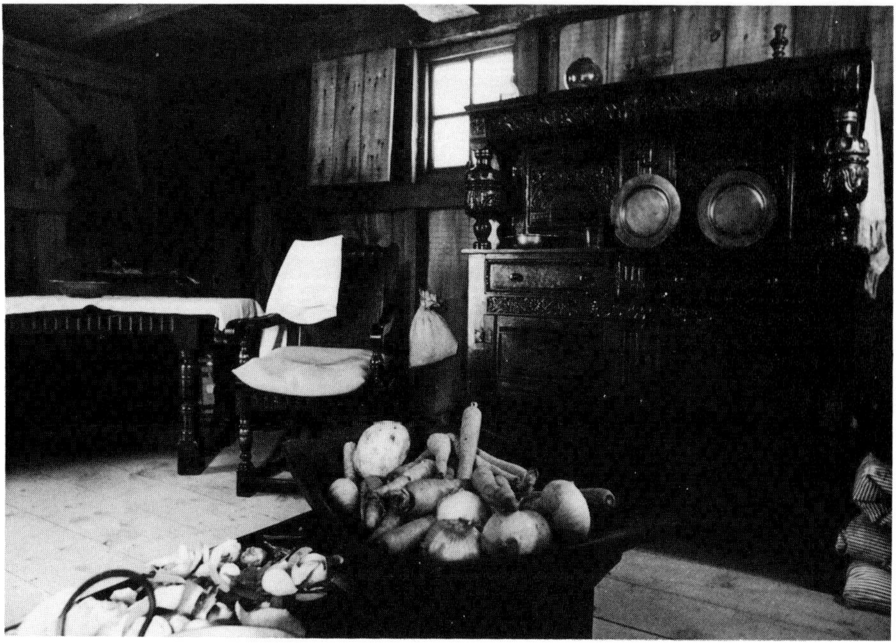

Courtesy of Plimoth Plantation

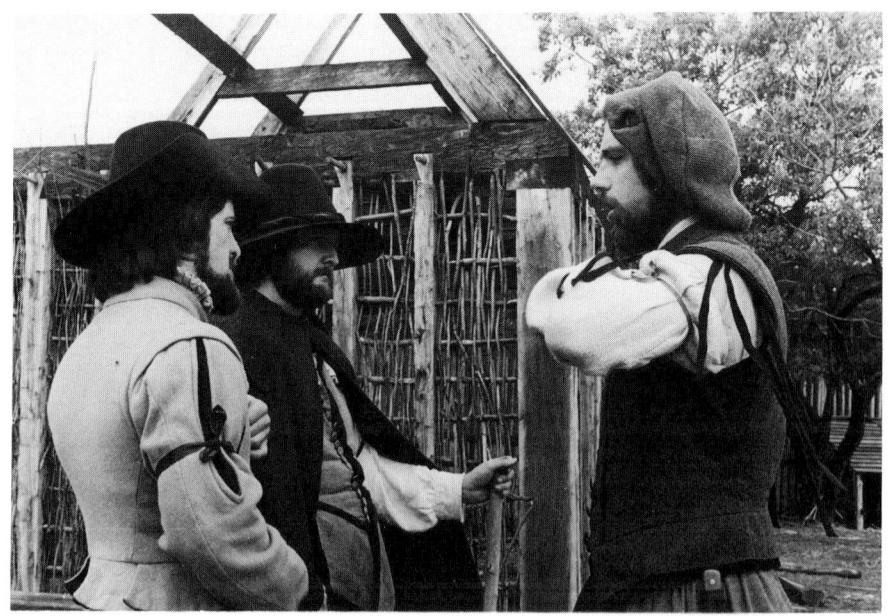

Interior of a house at Plimoth Plantation, as a Plymouth colony home might have appeared in 1627.

Courtesy of Plimoth Plantation

"Settlers" at Plimoth Plantation's re-creation of the Plymouth colony. Plymouth men, women and children wearing early 17th century styles re-create village life for visitors.

William Brewster wrote his name opposite the title page of a book he bought from William Peirse (or Peirce), a ship captain. Brewster noted that he bought the book of Peirse, cost 10/6, in Plimouth in New England, and wrote the motto *Hebel est omnis Adam* under his signature. Peirse's signature is at the top. The book also bears signatures of later owners; Alexander Standish bought it from Love Brewster. In the illustration below, part of the page was photographically enlarged and enhanced.

Robert B. Sherwood

Marker on land at Duxbury that Captain Myles Standish owned. The marker overlooks the water not far from Standish Street.

Elizabeth P. White
Courtesy of The Mayflower Quarterly

Robert B. Sherwood

Stone marking William Brewster's farm in Duxbury, Mass. It stands beside a road in the Nook, a peninsula.

Re-enactment of a Pilgrim procession during the 1981 Triennial Congress of the General Society of Mayflower Descendants in Plymouth, Mass. Representing Elder Brewster (center, with Bible) is Dwight Cushman, then Elder General of the Society. He is a descendant of Isaac Allerton and Richard Warren, who arrived on the *Mayflower*, and of Robert Cushman, the Pilgrims' agent in England.

In all, Brewster and Brewer published somewhere between 15 and 20 books before Dutch authorities, at the urging of the English ambassador, put them out of business.[43]

After the Ten Commandments book, the publishers issued two books in Latin, also in 1617. One was a reprint of a commentary on Proverbs, written by Thomas Cartwright, once a fellow of Peterhouse, Cambridge. It carried a preface written by the distinguished Dutch professor Johannes Polyander. The other book was a theological attack by Dr. William Ames against a scholar named Grevinchovius.

These books bore Brewster's Latinized name and address:

Apud Guiljelmum Brewsterum
In vico Chorali

All three books were safe, if somewhat dull by later standards.[44]

In a study entitled *The Pilgrim Press*, Rendel Harris and Stephen K. Jones come to the conclusion that the Dutch and Latin books bearing Brewster's name were issued as a cover for the real purpose of the press— to publish in English books of the type that had been prohibited in England and to distribute them clandestinely there. None of the English books known to have been printed at Choir Alley bear Brewster's name.[45] For that reason it is even more difficult now than it was in the days of James I to determine which of the prohibited books coming to the eyes of the English authorities were actually printed by Brewster.

The modern scholar, like the English authorities, may pore inconclusively over the books. A small emblem of a bear appears on ten of them. It is part of an old, larger woodcut, but its presence or absence is not considered proof of Choir Alley origin.[46]

Five books on which Brewster's name does not appear are attributed to the Choir Alley Press with some certainty. One of these was written by the Separatists' pastor, John Robinson, entitled *The People's Plea for the Exercise of Prophecying*. It was a defense of lay preaching. Another was Cartwright's *Confutation of the Remists'* [Roman] *Translation, Glosses &c of the New Testament*. Years later, Mrs. Robinson listed a copy of this book in her will.[47]

The small book which ended the whole publishing venture and sent Brewster into hiding may or may not have been printed by him. He never admitted it.

The book was the *Perth Assembly*, published in 1619. It was an attack on James I and the bishops of the Established Church in England. The author was David Calderwood, a leader in the Scots' independent Presbyterian Church which was still resisting the efforts of King James to impose English church uniformity in Scotland. Calderwood had eluded efforts by the English to capture him, and while hiding he wrote this book counselling the Scots to disregard the proceedings of the Assembly at Perth, Scotland. The Assembly had been called in 1618 by the hierarchy of the Established Church to crush opposition.[48]

The manuscript was smuggled to Holland and set in type there, either by Brewster or by some other printer with similar views. Copies of the book were secretly taken to Scotland, where they were popular and widely distributed. Inevitably some of the books fell into the hands of the authorities in England, and the hunt for the printer was on. Whether or not Brewster published the

Perth Assembly, it was in his library when he died in the Plymouth colony.[49]

Before the *Perth Assembly* affair, Brewster was busily supervising the operation of his publishing venture. The master printer was John Reynolds, brought over from London. His apprentice, who may have worked for Reynolds in London, was 22-year-old Edward Winslow. Winslow, originally from Droitwich in Worcestershire, would eventually sail on the *Mayflower* and become a leading member of the Plymouth colony.

Not long after their arrival in Leyden, both printers married English girls. Mary Brewster and her son Jonathan were among the witnesses to the betrothal of Reynolds to Prudence Grindon of London in August 1617. Jonathan's name on the document appears as Jonathan Willemsz (the Dutch version for William's son). Also listed as Jonathan Willemsz, he witnessed the betrothal of Apprentice Edward Winslow to Elizabeth Barker in April 1618.[50]

The Brewsters' house must have been a lively place in those years, with young children growing up, printers composing type in the garret, university students coming by for a lesson in English, church members consulting with Brewster on church business or personal problems. It all fell to pieces with the search for the printer of the *Perth Assembly*.

At about the same time that smuggled copies of the *Perth Assembly* were being seized by the King's men in Scotland, the English ambassador in the Netherlands, Sir Dudley Carleton, came across a copy there. He dutifully reported his efforts to find out who had published this book which held the King and the English bishops up to scorn. The ambassador wrote that he had been told it was printed by a certain English Brownist of Leyden.

He would obtain "more particular knowledge of the printer," he wrote to Secretary of State Sir Robert Naunton on July 17, 1619.[51]

Five days later he was writing another letter to Naunton:

"I sent your Honor a book intituled *Perth Assembly*, of which, finding many copies dispersed at Leyden and from thence sent into England, I had reason to suspect it was printed in that town; but upon more particular inquiry do rest somewhat doubtful. Yet in search after that book I believe I have discovered the printer of another, *De Regimine Ecclesiae Scoticanae*; which His Majesty was informed to be done at Middelburg; and that is one William Brewster, a Brownist, who hath been for some years an inhabitant and printer at Leyden; but is now within these three weeks removed from thence and gone back to dwell in London; where he may be found out and examined, not only of this book, *De Regimine Ecclesiae Scoticanae*, but likewise of *Perth Assembly*; of which, if he was not the printer himself, he assuredly knows both the printer and the author."[52]

Carleton enclosed the title page of still another book, which he said Brewster had admitted printing. The translation of its Latin title is *Concerning the true and genuine Religion of our Lord and Saviour Jesus Christ*. He also enclosed the title page of *De Regimine Ecclesiae Scoticanae*, a book critical of the English church hierarchy, declaring, "You will find that it is the same character." Since Brewster "doth openly avow" publication of the first, he could not well deny printing the second, the ambassador concluded.[53]

He probably hoped that his report that Brewster had

fled to London would end his own responsibility. It did not.

Secretary Naunton wrote back to the ambassador on August 3:

"I am told William Brewster is come again for Leyden; where I doubt not but your Lordship will lay for him if he come thither; as I will likewise do here; where I have already committed some of his complices and am commanded to make search for the rest."[54]

James I was clearly prodding his Secretary of State.

Naunton's letters include the mystifying report that "Brewster's son, of his fathers sect within this half year, now comes to Church." He adds that he "recovered" a note from Brewster to this son, and that he "committed the deliverer close until he discover where the father is." This hints at the existence of another Brewster son. Perhaps coincidentally, an Edward Brewster completed apprenticeship for the trade of printer in London in 1615; his first publication registered in 1616 was entitled *A Lowe Countrye Trayning*, and between 1616 and 1640 he published 25 books either reprinting sermons or concerning religious controversy. The "son" never appears again in the Pilgrim story.[55]

By August 20 the ambassador in the Netherlands wrote to Secretary Naunton: "I have made good inquiry after William Brewster, at Leyden, and am well assured that he is not returned thither; neither is it likely he will, having removed from thence both his family and goods."[56]

Naunton sent another diplomatic dispatch to the ambassador on August 23, instructing him that his Majesty desired the ambassador to "deal roundly" with the Dutch

States General in securing Brewster's arrest, if they valued his Majesty's friendship. Naunton believed that Brewster was still—or again—in Holland.[57]

The Dutch States General some time previously had issued an edict against unlicensed printing. Since at least some of Brewster's books were unlicensed, and since he had raised the wrath of the English King, the Dutch authorities raided the Brewsters' garret and seized the remaining books, type and printing equipment they found there. They affixed a big green wax seal across the closed garret door and hoped this would be an end of it.

However the Dutch cooperation with the English ambassador was questionable, at the least. One of the men designated to seize the books and type was Leyden University's Professor Polyander—who wrote the preface to one of the books printed by the Choir Alley Press.[58]

It seems clear that the Dutch could have arrested Brewster if they had wanted to.

By August 28 Ambassador Carleton was writing back to the Secretary of State: "Touching Brewster, I am now informed that he is on this side of the seas and was seen yesterday at Leyden, but as yet is not there settled."[59]

Less than a week later, Carleton was reporting that Brewster had been seen in Amsterdam, but he "is not as yet to be lighted upon." However, he added, "I understand he proposes to settle himself at a village called Leerdorp not far from Leyden, thinking there to be able to print prohibited books without discovery, but I shall lay wait for him both there and in other places, so as I doubt not but either he must leave this country; or I shall, sooner or later, find him out."[60]

Brave words, but someone was laying a wild goose trail.

Finally Carleton had something concrete to report. On September 9, the Leyden authorities questioned Thomas Brewer, Brewster's financial backer. Brewer said that he had discontinued the printing business in accordance with a proclamation about the publishing of unlicensed books. He added that his partner, William Brewster, was then in town, but that he was sick.

The next day, Carleton wrote in triumph to Naunton: "I have at Length found out Brewster at Leyden whom the magistrates of that town at my instance apprehended yesternight though he was sick in bed."[61]

Carleton's triumph was brief. On September 12, the ambassador was painfully writing a correction: "I advertised your Honor that Brewster was taken at Leyden: which proved an error in that the Scout who was employed by the magistrates for his apprehension being a dull, drunken fellow took one man for another."[62]

Most embarrassing! The pursuit of William Brewster was apparently abandoned after that.

However his partner, Thomas Brewer, had been detained and was being questioned. He said that the Choir Alley Press had published nothing since November 1618, which would have absolved the Press of issuing the *Perth Assembly.*

King James demanded that Brewer be sent to London for further questioning. The Leyden University authorities, who had jurisdiction since Brewer was connected with the university, refused to force him to return to England. Finally, after negotiations, Brewer agreed to return voluntarily to England, provided it would be for only a three-month period, and the King would bear the entire expense. He left in the custody of Sir William Zouch, a member of the Privy Council, who had been in Holland on other business.

They set out for the port of Flushing, where severe

storms kept them for several weeks before they could embark for England. Brewer's relationship with his custodian was friendly. Ambassador Carleton reported to London that the Leyden Brownists were somewhat scandalized to learn that Sir William Zouch had taught Brewer to drink *healths* while they waited for the weather to clear.[63]

Thomas Brewer gave the King little satisfaction when he was questioned in England, and was finally released with the expectation that he would return to Leyden "to do his utmost in finding out Brewster."[64] However King James refused to pay Brewer's passage back to Leyden, despite his pledge, and Brewer remained in England for three years. By the time Thomas Brewer returned to Leyden, William Brewster was in America.

It is a little easier for the modern historian to trace some of William Brewster's movements while he was a hunted man in 1619 than it was for the British ambassador. The Dutch never cooperated in the hunt. Brewer, Brewster, John Robinson, and Robinson's congregation were well liked in Leyden. The persecution of the publisher of a book on religion was contrary to the Dutch spirit of toleration. The author of *Perth Assembly*, David Calderwood, fled in August 1619 to Holland, where he found sanctuary. King James angrily called him "that knave who is now loupen over sea, with his purse well filled by the wives of Edinburgh."[65]

Brewster's master printer, John Reynolds, moved to Amsterdam and did not appear again in the Pilgrim story, but the apprentice, Edward Winslow, remained in Leyden.

While the pursuit of Printer William Brewster went on, Brewster had already ended for all time his printing activities. Instead he was deep in the preparations to found a colony of Separatists on the continent of America.

6   The Dream of America

FOR THE ENGLISH SEPARATISTS, life in Leyden was safe, with the exception of the trouble Brewster's printing had stirred up. Life was fairly comfortable, at the cost of long hours of work. The people had freedom of worship. And yet—

By 1617, the year Brewster began printing books, he was also conferring with Pastor John Robinson and leading laymen of the church about the possibility of transporting it to a new home somewhere in the vast New World.

They felt that their church in Leyden had reached the peak of its growth there, and that their religion and culture were in danger of being gradually assimilated into the Dutch community.

There was danger too of a renewal of the war with Spain. The peace the Dutch were enjoying was only a truce, and the truce was due to expire in 1621. Brewster had seen the ravages of war in the Netherlands during his service there with Davison. All the English in Leyden knew from their Dutch neighbors of the terrible Spanish siege of Leyden, now nearly forty years ago. They knew about the famine, the children weakened by hunger dying of the diseases that accompany war, the Spanish demands for surrender which were always rejected. They knew about the sound of rushing waters as the Dutch forces cut the dikes and sailed their food-laden ships through them with a gale at their backs to relieve the survivors of the siege.

(War was in fact renewed in 1621. By that time, Spain was already fighting against France, Sweden and several German States in the Thirty Years War. The Thirty Years War was concluded in the 1648 Treaty of Westphalia, in which Spain recognized the independence of the United Netherlands.)

During the early years of the Leyden church, more Separatists from England and members of the Amsterdam churches had occasionally come to Leyden, but now this immigration had virtually ceased. Only the hardiest were able to work the long hours necessary to provide the mere essentials for a family. For themselves, the Leyden church members could bear such privation, but they winced at the realization that constant, grinding labor was robbing their older children of their youthful strength and joy. Worse yet from the parents' viewpoint, some of the children rebelled against this austere life and left the community to become Dutch soldiers or sailors or to follow courses which their church considered corrupt.

Once the decision to relocate had been made, Brewster, Robinson and the other "sagest leaders" decided that the American continent, or perhaps one of its offshore islands, offered the best possibility. They wanted room for expansion, opportunity to earn a living, and remoteness from oppressive authority. Methodically, they pored over the books which told of the New World with varying degrees of accuracy.

Always an avid book buyer, Brewster had several of

these books in his own library. One known as Hakluyt's *Navigations* included an account of Sir Francis Drake's expedition around the earth.

Captain John Smith's *Description of New England* was just off the press in 1616, and the Leyden English studied it in detail. They were encouraged by Smith's conclusion that "Worthy is that person to starve that here cannot live if he have sense, strength, and health." Smith included a map in his book, as well as other extremely useful information. In 1619 Smith himself offered to act as a guide to the Pilgrims, but they turned down his offer, probably because of their precarious financial position, or because of a commitment to Myles Standish. Smith's experience might well have helped through the first winter. He said as much later: "Their humorous ignorances caused them for more than a year to endure a wonderful deal of misery with infinite patience."[1]

Both Smith's and Hakluyt's books were in Brewster's Plymouth library at the time of his death. He probably carried them with him aboard the *Mayflower* along with a number of others.

Brewster and his friends also studied the writings of Sir Walter Raleigh. His *Discovery of Guiana* painted an alluring picture of the South American land between the Orinoco and the Amazon rivers, a land of rich plains with fine grass, beautiful hills, flourishing groves, gentle deer, sweetly singing birds, possible mineral deposits. Sir Walter called it "a region which I am resolved cannot be equalled, for health, air, riches, pleasure, by any region either east or west."[2]

Guiana's warm climate and plentiful food had a strong appeal to some of the Leyden congregation, but the decision finally went against settling there. The Spanish were close and might seize an English colony, especially if it appeared to be prospering. True, the climate was warm, but hot countries were known to be "subject to grievous diseases," Bradford wrote. The conditions in such a climate would "not so well agree with our English bodies," he added.[3]

The Pilgrims' misgivings about Guiana were confirmed by Raleigh himself. In 1617 he led an expedition to South America on a mission to locate a gold mine he said he had found on his earlier exploration in 1595. By the time his ship sailed away from the Orinoco river, Raleigh and many of his crew were desperately ill, his fleet had been battered by storms, and one of his captains had deserted him. Armed Spaniards were waiting for the landing party and Raleigh's son was killed. The British burned the Spanish settlement, and they found no gold mine. The expedition was a disaster.

English people were already living in the colony of Virginia, but there was the likelihood that if the Pilgrims were to settle there too, English authority might harass the Separatist Church, and its members would be no better off than they had been in England.

But perhaps they might settle some way off, as a distinct body, under the general government of Virginia. This was the final decision, and preparations to secure permission for such a colony were soon under way.

The obstacles were great. The emigrating members of the church would liquidate their assets, but that would not provide enough money to outfit the journey. Their hope was to interest one of the English commercial companies in staking the venture as an investment, with the expectation that it would be profitable. They also needed permission from the English authorities—ultimately from King James himself—to colonize.

William Brewster dipped his pen in ink and drafted

a letter to a man he had known since the Scrooby days—
Sir Edwin Sandys. Sandys, about six years older than
Brewster, was the son of Brewster's old landlord at
Scrooby Manor, Archbishop Sandys. Edwin Sandys had
been a member of Parliament since 1586. On the accession of James I, Edwin Sandys was knighted along with
countless others, although he subsequently became the
object of royal displeasure. He often pressed causes the
King disliked: He tried to secure for all prisoners the
right to employ counsel; he declared that there were con-
stitutional limits to the power of both the King and the
people; he was briefly imprisoned in 1621, suspected of
plotting to establish a republican government in the Virginia colony; he successfully led the opposition to the
union of Scotland and England which the King wanted.

But at the point he enters the Pilgrim story, Sir Edwin
Sandys was an influential man in Parliament, an aristo-
crat with a trim white beard who posed for his portrait
wearing a wide lace collar. He was interested in exploration and colonization, and he was a Puritan sympathizer.
Since 1607 he had been a member of the Council for
the Virginia Company, which was financing the Virginia
colony, and in 1617 he became the Council's joint man-
ager with the Earl of Southampton (Shakespeare's patron).

The Virginia Company charter went as far north as 41
degrees latitude, the vicinity of Manhattan Island. At
the time the Pilgrims were seeking to settle in the New
World, the Virginia Company occasionally granted large
tracts of land to groups who would settle and cultivate
them, with the right to local self-government, and the
Pilgrims were interested in such an arrangement.[4]

In the summer of 1617, the Leyden Separatists sent
two of their agents to talk with the Virginia Council.

They probably carried a letter signed by Pastor John Robinson and William Brewster.

The Pilgrims' first "ambassadors" were two deacons of the church, John Carver and Robert Cushman.

Carver was married to Robinson's sister-in-law, Catherine. She had been a widow when he married her, and he had been skillful in the management of the estate she had inherited from her first husband. Carver first appears in the church records at Leyden in 1616, so he must have gained rapid recognition. The Pilgrims apparently trusted both his judgment and his honesty. He had once been a merchant in Doncaster, England.

Cushman's honesty was never attacked, but the Leyden leaders constantly found fault with his judgment, to the point that he was sickened by it. He was a wool comber, originally from Canterbury. His wife and one of their two children died in 1616. Not long after, he remarried, and within a few months of the marriage he left for England on his mission for the church, leaving his nine-year-old son and his new wife in Leyden. He spent most of the next three years in England, torn between the demands of the English there who might back the venture and the conditions to which the Pilgrims could agree.[5]

William Brewster also made one or more trips to England to help in the negotiations, although by 1619 he discreetly kept out of sight of officials who were then seeking to arrest him for printing prohibited books. His name appears prominently and openly in the early negotiations, dwindles to "Mr. B." in a letter from Cushman to the Leyden congregation, and finally disappears altogether as the hunt for the printer intensified.[6]

He probably kept moving from safe house to safe house. Cushman makes a vague reference that Brewster might go "to the north."[7] Perhaps he stayed with sympathizers who would have gone to Leyden earlier if they had been younger or their health better, or who had lived in Leyden for a time but had returned to England. Most of the Leyden English had relatives still in England who could have sheltered Brewster for a few nights. Edward Winslow, Brewster's printer, had brothers living in Worcestershire. One of them later went aboard the *Mayflower* at Southampton, and three others eventually emigrated to the Plymouth colony.

The Aldgate ward in the East End of old London was a center for nonconformist church activity at this period, according to Charles Edward Banks (*The English Ancestry and Homes of the Pilgrim Fathers*). Edward Southworth and his wife Alice lived there in the Duke's Place in a tenement called Heneage House, which had been the town palace of an abbot. The Southworths had lived in Leyden for a time, then moved back to London. Aldgate was the home of hundreds of Dutch craftsmen, the site of a Dutch church. Many of its English residents had the same family names as a number of the *Mayflower* passengers—Allerton, Tilley, Sampson, Hopkins, etc. William Bradford's name appears on the tax rolls in March 1620 as taxed for personal property in the Duke's Place. Evidently Bradford was there for a short time helping with the final preparations for the voyage. (Edward Southworth remained in London and died there a few years later; in 1623 his widow Alice married Bradford, who was by then a widower himself.)[8]

In the negotiations about a colony, the envoys, Carver and Cushman, were encouraged by Sandys and the other members of the Virginia Company. They were willing to grant the settlers a patent to colonize, and set about getting the King's approval, which they thought likely.

The sticking point, of course, was the insistence on freedom of worship, the cause for which they had fled to Holland. Sandys asked Carver and Cushman to obtain from the Leyden church a statement of the principles which would be guiding their church in the New World. It would have to contain reference to their acceptance of the King's authority, and it would have to be phrased in a manner that would win his approval of the settlement without jettisoning everything for which the church members had struggled.

Robinson and Brewster struggled over this assignment, finally drafting a brief set of principles which they called the "Seven Articles." As required, they acknowledged the King as supreme governor in his dominion in all causes and over all persons. They accepted obedience to the King's authority, but added a qualification, "if the thing commanded be not against God's Word."[9]

Robinson and Brewster signed their names to the Seven Articles, and Carver and Cushman submitted them to Sandys and the rest of the Council. So far as the Articles went—and they certainly glossed over the Separatists' views—they were satisfactory to the Council.

Cushman and Carver left England for Leyden to report to the church, bringing with them a letter dated November 12, 1617, from Sir Edwin Sandys to John Robinson and William Brewster. Sandys gave Robinson and Brewster hope, but cautioned that the matter was still under discussion. He signed his letter, "Your very loving friend."[10]

So there it stood. Robinson and Brewster decided to write another letter to Sandys, less formal than the Seven Articles, but truly descriptive of the spirit guiding the little group of petitioners. Because this letter sheds more light on the Pilgrims' motivation and courage than any other document, it seems worthwhile to quote liberally from it. The writers list five points which set forth their motives:

"1. We verily believe and trust the Lord is with us, unto whom and whose service we have given ourselves in many trials; and that He will graciously prosper our endeavours according to the simplicity of our hearts therein.

"2. We are well weaned from the delicate milk of our mother country, and inured to the difficulties of a strange and hard land, which yet in a great part we have by patience overcome.

"3. The people are, for the body of them, industrious and frugal, we think we may safely say, as any company of people in the world.

"4. We are knit together as a body in a most strict and sacred bond and covenant of the Lord, of the violation whereof we make great conscience, and by virtue whereof we do hold ourselves straitly tied to all care of each other's good and of the whole, by every one and so mutually.

"5. Lastly, it is not with us as with other men, whom small things can discourage, or small discontentments cause to wish themselves at home again. We know our entertainment in England and in Holland. We shall much prejudice both our arts and means by removal; who, if we should be driven to return, we should not hope to recover our present helps and comforts, neither indeed look ever, for ourselves, to attain unto the like in any other place during our lives, which are now drawing toward their periods.

"These motives we have been bold to tender unto

you, which you in your wisdom may also impart to
any other our worshipful friends of the Council with
you; of all whose godly disposition and loving toward
our despised persons we are most glad, and shall not
fail by all good means to continue and increase the
same. We will not be further troublesome, but do,
with the renewed remembrance of our humble duties
to your Worship and (so far as in modesty we may be
bold) to any other of our wellwillers of the Council
with you, we take our leaves, committing your
persons and counsels to the guidance and direction
of the Almighty.

Yours much bounden in all duty,

Leyden, December 15   John Robinson
Anno: 1617   William Brewster"[11]

The English at Leyden had established an excellent
reputation among the Dutch. The merchants of Leyden
were willing to trust them in any matter involving money
because they had found them careful to keep their word
and "painful and diligent in their callings." Bradford
wrote, "Yea, they would strive to get their custom and
to employ them above others in their work, for their
honesty and diligence."[12]

He also cited the comments of Dutch magistrates in a
case involving another group of immigrants, the French-
speaking Walloons. Bradford quoted the Dutch magistrates: "These English, said they, have lived amongst
us now these twelve years, and yet we never had any
suit or accusation come against any of them; but your
strifes and quarrels are continual, etc."[13]

In London Carver and Cushman pressed their cause
with a number of members of the Virginia Council as
well as with other men in a position of influence. They

were given great hope when Sir Robert Naunton, the Secretary of State (the same man who directed the hunt for Brewster in the printing matter), agreed to bring up the petition with the King. Naunton told the King that the colonists would attempt to advance his Majesty's dominions and enlarge the Gospel; the King looked down his long nose and said this was a good and honest motion.

"By what means will they exist there?" his Majesty asked.

"By fishing," Naunton answered.

"Fishing," James repeated. "So God have my soul, 'tis an honest trade. 'Twas the Apostles' own calling."[14]

The King preferred the smell of fish to the smell of Raleigh's tobacco, the principal export of Virginia, where Raleigh had been an active colonizer. Of smoking tobacco, his Majesty wrote: "A custom lothsome to the eye, hateful to the nose, harmfull to the braine, dangerous to the lungs, and in the black stinking fume therof, neerest resembling the horrible Stigian smoke of the pit that is bottomless."[15]

The King's attack on tobacco may have been an oblique attack on Raleigh himself. James had Raleigh confined to the Tower during most of his reign and finally had him executed.

The pleasant conversation about fishing between the King and Secretary of State Naunton took place before Naunton learned of the printing activities of one of the principal leaders of the Leyden congregation, William Brewster. However there is no indication that Naunton discouraged the colonization plans, even while he was urging his ambassador in Holland to secure Brewster's arrest. This was not inconsistent. Many years earlier, proposals had been made that troublesome Englishmen be sent to settle other places in the realm, where they might be less trouble . . . Ireland maybe.

Throughout the winter of 1617-18, the Leyden congregation's emissaries shuttled across the English channel, bearing letters between the Virginia Council and Leyden.

Sir John Wolstenholme, a member of the Virginia Council, asked for a more detailed explanation of the congregation's religious practices, to satisfy some of the King's Privy Council.

In a letter of February 6, 1618, Brewster and Robinson wrote that they enclosed two declarations, and that Wolstenholme might choose which to submit to the Privy Council members.[16] (Wolstenholme's contemporaries variously spelled his name Worstenholme and Worsenham.)

The first declaration was completely lacking in detail:

"Touching the ecclesiastical ministry, namely of pastors for teaching, elders for ruling, and deacons for distributing the church's contribution, as also for the two sacraments, baptism and the Lord's Supper, we do wholly and in all points agree with the French Reformed Churches, according to their public confession of faith.

"The oath of Supremacy we shall willingly take if it be required of us, and that convenient satisfaction be not given by our taking the oath of Allegiance."

The second version was about three times as long and cited what appear at this distance to be rather trivial distinctions between the practices of the Leyden church and the French Reformed churches, such as the point that "their ministers do pray with their heads covered; ours uncovered."

The desire of course was to minimize in the minds of the English authorities, and especially in the mind of the King, the differences between the Leyden church and the Established Church of England.

Robinson and Brewster signed both versions and handed them or sent them by someone else to a new messenger in England, Sabine Staresmore. For some reason they did not show Staresmore copies of the letters he was carrying, which put him at somewhat of a disadvantage. He took the letters to Wolstenholme and stood by while he read them. Wolstenholme "stuck" at some of the points in the Robinson-Brewster letter, and put some questions to Staresmore, who answered as well as he could without having read the letter.

Concerning the ordination of ministers, Wolstenholme asked, "Who shall make them?"

Staresmore replied, "The power of making is in the church, to be ordained by the imposition of hands by the fittest instruments they had."

This appeared not to satisfy Wolstenholme, so Staresmore continued that the power of ordination must either be in the church or from the Pope, and the Pope was Antichrist.

"Ho," countered Wolstenholme, "what the Pope holds good (as in the Trinity) that we do well to assent to. But we will not enter into dispute now." He told Staresmore that he thought it best not to show either of the letters to others "lest he should spoil all." Wolstenholme was disappointed that the letters did not agree with the Archbishop of Canterbury's views on the calling of ministers.

Nevertheless, he told Staresmore that both the King and the bishops had consented to the Leyden congregation's petition to colonize, a report that turned out to be too optimistic.[17]

Staresmore met with the group's chief patron, Sir Edwin Sandys, and attended a meeting of the Virginia Council.

Although King James had appeared to encourage the colonization plans when Sir Robert Naunton, his Secretary of State, brought up the matter, the King later told Naunton that the petitioners should confer with the Archbishop of Canterbury and the Bishop of London. However, as Winslow later put it, they decided to "persist upon his first approbation" and not entangle themselves with the bishops.

Some of their supporters did try to win the Archbishop's approval without success. It was clear that the King was unwilling to give his explicit permission to what the Leyden congregation most wanted, the right to their own form of religious worship. However, the Pilgrims concluded, they might be able to achieve their aim anyway.

Bradford wrote:

"Yet thus far they prevailed, in sounding his Majesty's mind, that he would connive at them and not molest them, provided they carried themselves peaceably. But to allow or tolerate them by his public authority, under his seal, they found it would not be. And this was all the chief of the Virginia Company or any other of their best friends could do in the case. Yet they persuaded them to go on, for they presumed they should not be troubled."[18]

The messengers carried this advice back to the Leyden congregation. It was the best they could do, but it was far from satisfactory. In Bradford's words, "This made a damp in the business."

Some members of the Leyden church feared that the

opposition of the English bishops and lack of the King's express approval might crumble the foundation of their efforts to emigrate. Perhaps they should never have tried to win the King's tolerance for their non-conformist church.

The final decision, however, was to proceed with their plan, on the assumption that the King was willing to accept the plan, even though he was not willing to say so publicly. Furthermore, they grimly concluded, even a public promise could not be relied upon. Bradford wrote, ". . . for if afterwards there should be a purpose or desire to wrong them, though they had a seal as broad as the house floor it would not serve the turn; for there would be means enow found to recall or reverse it."[19]

They determined to put their faith in the providence of God and remain on their chosen course.

Messengers from the Leyden congregation shuttled between Leyden and the Virginia Council during 1618 and 1619. The atmosphere in England toward dissent with the throne was not encouraging. Many Englishmen who remembered Sir Walter Raleigh's days of glory and bold exploration under Queen Elizabeth were shocked when King James ordered Raleigh's execution in October 1618, although Raleigh was never a popular favorite. Raleigh had been under sentence of death on a trumped-up charge of treason since the first part of James's reign. He was released from the Tower in 1616 to conduct the ill-starred treasure hunt up the Orinoco river, but returned to England without treasure. His men had fought against the Spanish at a time when Spain and England were not at war and at a time when James hoped to marry his son Charles to a Spanish princess. James called this a crime worthy of death.

The accusations against Raleigh included a charge

that he intended to start war between the Kings of England and Spain. He was also charged with abusing his Majesty's commission. This last was reminiscent of the accusation against William Davison after he sent the death warrant of Mary Queen of Scots to Fotheringhay castle.

James was not a popular King although he had maintained a policy of peace and was somewhat of an intellectual. People far more worldly than the Pilgrims found his personal habits and his associates disgusting. James was physically unattractive, particularly to people who were old enough to remember the Gloriana splendor of Elizabeth. He drooled; his legs seemed too thin to support his weight; he leaned against things and often fell down. He had read widely and was interested in theology, but his discourse was garrulous, sometimes silly. He was not convincing in his argument of the divine right of kings.

The Pilgrims would have looked with dismay upon the declaration James issued in 1618, in which he ordered that on Sundays, after the Divine Service, people should not be barred from taking part in sports, dancing and other harmless recreation. He specifically stated that they should be permitted May-games, Whitsun ales, Morris dances and May poles.[20] One of the reasons the Separatists wanted to leave Holland was that the Dutch took part in similar recreation on Sundays and set a bad example for the Separatists' children. The Sabbath, to the Separatists, was for worship and rest.

In mid-1618 some of the always troublesome Ancient Brethren from Amsterdam made a decision of their own to go to Virginia and came to London to make arrangements. Again, they brought trouble with them. Their leader, Elder Francis Blackwell, was arrested when a meeting at a private house in London was raided by authorities. He managed to escape prison by telling the officials where they could find Sabine Staresmore, who had escaped from the meeting. Blackwell talked his own way out, mainly by incriminating Staresmore, who was thrown in prison. Another visiting Leyden church member, Richard Masterson, escaped only because Blackwell did not know where he was staying in London.

Staresmore, the Leyden messenger who had delivered the letters to Sir John Wolstenholme a few months earlier, wrote a pitiful letter from prison to John Carver dated September 4, 1618. He told Carver of his petitions for release from prison in which he pointed out "that I was a young man living by my credit, indebted to divers in our city, living at more than ordinary charges in a close and tedious prison, besides great rents abroad, all my business lying still, my only servant lying lame in the country, my wife being also great with child."[21]

While Staresmore languished in prison, Blackwell, always a fast talker, managed to secure dismissal of charges against himself as well as the Archbishop's blessing for his plans to sail for Virginia. It is not known how long Staresmore remained in prison; eventually he returned to Leyden but did not accompany the Pilgrims to America. In 1622 he became a member of Ainsworth's church in Amsterdam.

Blackwell, however, set sail for Virginia on a ship with 180 persons "packed together like herrings." Strong winds carried them out of their course. Their supplies of water ran low. Most of the crew and passengers became ill, and day after day, people were dying. The captain and six of his crew died, and the remaining mariners were for a time unable to find the bay they were seeking. Blackwell himself died. In the end 130 of the 180 who sailed aboard the ship were dead by the time the ship finally reached its Virginia port in March of 1619.[22]

Samuel Argall, Deputy Governor of Virginia, brought the news of the Blackwell group's disaster back to England with him. It would add to the anxiety which the Leyden emigrants felt as they turned their own faces toward the harsh Atlantic sea. Robert Cushman, writing from London with news of the Blackwell venture, commented, "Heavy news it is, and I would be glad to hear how far it will discourage. I see none here discouraged much, but rather desire to learn to beware by other men's harms and to amend that wherein they have failed."

Cushman added, "It is as Mr. Robinson once said— he thought we should hear no good of them."[23]

Bradford sternly wrote, "If such events follow the bishops' blessing, happy are they that miss the same."[24]

The men and women who were to be known as the Pilgrims were not easily discouraged.

A new obstacle appeared. The Virginia Company was so torn with dissension and financial troubles that it was unable to act on the colonization plan. A faction headed by Sir Edwin Sandys, Brewster's patron, achieved Sandys' election as treasurer of the Virginia Council in 1619, replacing Sir Thomas Smith, who had been treasurer for twelve years.

The election was not pleasing to King James, who considered Sandys an enemy. Later, when Sandys was up for re-election to the Council post, James cried, "Choose the devil if you will, but not Sir Edwin Sandys."[25]

Even after Sandys' 1619 election, a faction headed by Smith, the unsuccessful candidate, carried on a running battle with Sandys and those who supported him.

Throughout all these troubles, the emissaries of the Leyden congregation continued to work for the issuance of a patent which would give them the right to settle in a specific part of the American wilderness. Brewster was one of them in 1619, shortly before the King's men began their hunt for him as the printer of the *Perth Assembly*. Even before the hunt began, he played an inconspicuous though important role. Robert Cushman continued to write the official reports on negotiations, addressing them to the Leyden congregation, while Brewster, sometimes travelling outside London, wrote to Pastor Robinson personally.

By July Brewster was being sought both in England and in Holland as the printer of prohibited books. His name appeared on no further communications from Leyden, and Cushman did not mention him again in his own letters, which could have been seized.

Even before the *Perth Assembly*, the Leyden church members had been advised by their friends on the Virginia Council not to use the names of any of their own members in applying for a patent. They finally used the name of John Wincop, a tutor or chaplain in the house of the Dowager Countess of Lincoln. A patent was granted in his name June 9, 1619, but it was never used. Wincop had intended to accompany the colonizers but he did not emigrate.[26]

The Wincop patent, however, encouraged the Leyden church members in their planning. Pastor John Robinson called his flock together for one of the gatherings they customarily held to consider serious matters—a solemn meeting and a day of humiliation to ask the Lord for his direction. Robinson preached to them from a Biblical text which read, "And David's men said unto him, see we be afraid here in Judah, how much more if we come to Keilah against the host of the Philistines? Then David asked counsel of the Lord again." (I Samuel 23:3,4.)[27]

Pilgrims' own faith

The pastor's words and their own faith in what they regarded as a mission in accordance with the will of God gave them courage to persist in the face of obstacles. The Bible passage from which Robinson quoted read further, "And the Lord answered him, and said, Arise, go down to Keilah; for I will deliver the Philistines into thine hand."

They realized that all the members could not go at once for a number of practical reasons. Therefore, the congregation would split into two separate churches until they might be united again. The larger number, though not much larger, would stay in Leyden for the present, and their pastor, John Robinson, would stay with them. William Brewster would be the head of the church to be formed in America. He would continue to be their elder, but not their pastor. They expected that John Robinson would come to them shortly. Nevertheless, until the church in America could have an ordained minister, Brewster would be responsible for the church, preaching its sermons, correcting wayward members, performing all the functions of a pastor except for administering the sacraments.

As soon as others could, they would come to America, where they would be made welcome. On the other hand any colonists who returned to Leyden could immediately take their place again in their old church. This provision for contingencies brought some peace of mind.

While negotiations dragged on in London, Pastor Robinson in Leyden received a tentative offer from Dutch traders to take the Separatists to the Dutch trading post on Manhattan Island. The prospects were attractive— free transport, cattle, protection as long as needed, and best of all, the right to self-government in internal affairs. Amsterdam merchants who backed the proposal applied on February 12, 1620, to the Stadtholder for assurances of the military protection for such a colony, initially that two warships should be sent out to secure provisionally the lands to the Dutch government. The States-General turned down the request on April 11. However by that time the members of the Leyden congregation were deep in planning with Thomas Weston, a London merchant adventurer who was long a part of the Pilgrim story.

Weston was a business man with a finger in many pots. He was a London ironmonger originally, later a promoter involved in unlicensed trade with the Netherlands and eventually a planter and burgess in Virginia. He operated just inside the law on some occasions and outside it on others. He was a persuasive man and he came to Leyden at a time when negotiations were dragging.

Weston put new life into the project. Forget the Dutch offer for transportation to Manhattan Island, he advised them. Do not depend too much on the Virginia Company. If they fail you, Weston said, he and his friends would provide capital for their venture. The English at Leyden should speedily wind up their preparations, and he would take care of raising the money.

He wanted something in writing, to show his fellow investors in England, so the colonists should draw up an agreement satisfactory to them, which he would then present to the group eventually known in Bradford's history as the Adventurers.

The agreement was drawn up. Weston went off with it to London. Those who were to go to America began to sell their houses and decide what they could take with them.

The news from London was good. Weston formed a joint stock company of 70 investors who put up seven thousand pounds. He anticipated a profit from the hunting and fishing the colony would carry on, with half the profit to go to the Adventurers and half to the settlers.

However the terms of the agreement soon began to slip. Carver and Cushman in England were instructed to provide for shipping, receive money from the Adventurers, and buy provisions for the journey. They were not authorized to change the agreement, and were indeed expressly forbidden to "exceed the bounds of your commission."[28]

Nevertheless Weston, saying that the other Adventurers demanded changes, presented the Pilgrim agents with a revised agreement. There were two important changes. The settlers had originally agreed to work five days a week for the benefit of the entire company, and save two days for their own needs. This was changed to require them to work seven days a week for the common interests. Originally, the houses which the settlers would build and their gardens were to belong to the settlers who built them. This was changed to include the homes and surrounding ground in the general property of the company, to be divided at the end of seven years according to the number of shares a shareholder held.

Carver and Cushman reluctantly agreed to the new agreement, although letters from the Netherlands sharply told them that they had no authority to do so. The new terms were repugnant to the Leyden English. Bradford Smith, in his excellent biography of William Bradford, *Bradford of Plymouth*, suggests that a yearning for land was one of the motives for the colonization, as many of the Scrooby people had farmed in England. Further, the change in the agreement implied a change in social status, the matter of "degree" that was important to these Englishmen despite their insistence on equality for all in the sight of God. These new conditions, they complained, were "fitter for thieves and bondslaves than honest men." They were being committed to work for seven years without wages, the status of indentured servants. Why, they demanded, should they be planning to take servants to work for them since the new agreement would put all in the status of servants?[29]

Anguished letters went back and forth across the channel during the month of June 1620. Cushman, who bore the brunt of the displeasure, protested that the Adventurers would have withdrawn if he had not agreed to the changes. In the matter of home ownership, he wrote that the settlers should not plan to build valuable houses. The purpose, he wrote, "is to build for the present such houses as, if need be, we may with little grief set afire and run away by the light."[30]

Robinson, usually a man of great patience, wrote a letter to Carver, his brother-in-law, fairly boiling over with exasperation at Cushman. Cushman, he said, "is known (though a good man and of special abilities in his kind) yet most unfit to deal for other men by reason of his singularity and too great indifferency for any conditions."[31]

This was the most disturbing time in the life of the Leyden church. Some withdrew from the venture; others would have done so if they had not already sold their property and committed their funds. Even the exact destination was still uncertain. Weston now was urging New England, on a grant of land derived out of the Virginia patent but apart from its government.

Brewster was still in hiding because of the *Perth Assembly* publication, and his conciliating presence was missed.

His financial backer in the printing business, Thomas

Brewer, was now in England and at liberty. He was one of the investors in the Adventurers' undertaking.

Cushman in London and Carver in the port of Southampton quarrelled between themselves over the preparations for the voyage. Although Cushman addressed a letter to Carver, "To his loving friend Mr. John Carver," the letter complained that Carver had wrongly accused him of negligence. "I marvel why so negligent a man was used in the business," Cushman said coldly.[32]

In buying provisions for the voyage and making other preparations, Cushman and Carver were joined by a new figure, a trouble-maker as it turned out. Since there were not enough of the Leyden group able to sail immediately for America, a miscellaneous group of about 80 English men and women had been recruited by the Adventurers to fill the ranks. They were not Separatists, although many of them eventually joined the Pilgrim church. Some of them had skills which were useful in the new colony. Most of them were unacquainted with the others. Still, the Adventurers demanded and the Leyden people agreed that a representative of the new group should also be named to share in the preparations. The man chosen by the Adventurers was Christopher Martin, a Puritan who was born at Great Burstead, Essex.

Martin proceeded to Kent on a buying trip, while Carver was laying in other provisions at Southampton, the port from which they planned to sail. Cushman was in London with Weston. The agents criticized each other's actions and as Cushman pointed out, "we are readier to go to dispute than to set forward a voyage."[33]

Despite all the obstacles and personality clashes, plans for the voyage began to converge.

A ship was hired, the *Speedwell,* a 60-ton pinnace which
the colonists hoped to keep in the New World as a fishing
vessel, although none of them had ever fished. It was re-
fitted in Delft Haven in the Netherlands. From Delft
Haven it would carry the Leyden people to join the English contingent in Southampton. The extensive repair
work it needed added to the financial burden.

Although the Leyden church members had never met
most of the settlers who would be joining them at Southampton, Pastor Robinson and perhaps the others as well
knew Myles Standish, who would be in charge of their
defenses. Standish had served with the English troops
during the period just before they finally were withdrawn from the Netherlands. The English from Scrooby
were living in Amsterdam, preparing to move to Leyden,
at that time. Somewhere, the paths of the Pilgrim pastor
and the young English officer crossed. More than a
decade later, Standish was packing up weapons and a
supply of ammunition for use, if needed, in the new colony's defense.

He was always known as the Captain. Standish was
short, with a florid complexion which reddened even
more when he was angered. And he was easily provoked to anger. During the early years at Plymouth,
after Standish and others had killed several Indians in a
skirmish, Robinson wrote to Governor Bradford, "Consider of the disposition of your Captain, whom I love,
and am persuaded the Lord in great mercy and for much
good hath sent you him, if you use him aright." Robinson warned that although Standish was "humble and
meek" toward all in the ordinary course of events, nevertheless, if provoked, he might lack "tenderness of the life
of man."[34]

No one ever questioned Standish's courage or his loyalty. His little Pilgrim army never suffered defeat. Although he was a leader in the Plymouth colony, he never joined its church. He attended it and declared himself in favor of religious toleration.

Standish was 36 years old when he and his wife Rose packed their belongings and said goodbye to their relatives and friends in Lancashire, England.

The packing was a difficult business for everybody. They all knew that space aboard ship was limited, but that on the other hand they would have to take with them everything they expected to need for at least a year—clothing, cooking utensils, tools, medical supplies, guns, bedding and the rest.

Brewster insisted on taking his books. The Brewster family, like many others, was leaving some of its members to come on a later ship. William and Mary were taking the two youngest children, Love, who was ten years old, and Wrestling, who was six. Jonathan would remain behind for the time being, working at his trade as a ribbon maker and living in a tiny cottage behind the Robinsons. His wife and child had died only a year earlier. Patience, aged 20, and Fear, now 14, were staying in Leyden too, probably with the Robinson's big family. The Robinsons also had a little girl named Fear, which may have caused some confusion. It was a fairly common practice then in England, especially among the upper classes, to send a child to live for a time with family friends.

It was also a common practice to assign poor orphan children to live with more prosperous families—not as adopted children, but as servants, who as they grew up would be expected to work for their keep. They would be indentured servants, and when their indentures ended, they would be free agents. It has long been assumed that this was the reason why a little boy named Richard More, about six years old, and his brother or sister were "put to" the family of William and Mary Brewster, to live with them in the New World. Another More boy, Jasper, was "put to" John and Catherine Carver, and little Ellen More was assigned to Edward Winslow and his young wife.

An English genealogist, Sir Anthony Wagner, has discovered that the More children were not orphans, but had been abandoned by their prominent family. The discovery reveals an old scandal. Catherine More, 23, heiress to the estate of Larden, was married in 1610 to her third cousin, 16-year-old Samuel More, probably with the aim of keeping the estate in the family. Four children listed as the children of Samuel More were baptized at Shipton between 1612 and 1616. Three of the names are the same as those of the More children listed by Bradford as *Mayflower* passengers. The fourth was Mary. Bradford said a brother of Richard More sailed with the Brewsters, but it probably was four-year-old Mary.

However Samuel More (or Moore) was apparently not the father of the children. In a declaration made to the Lord Chief Justice of England in or about 1620, More said that the children had been baptized as his before he realized "the common fame of the adulterous life of the said Katherine More with one Jacob Blakeway, a fellow of mean parentage and condition." Furthermore, he pointed out, there was "apparent likeness and resemblance of most of the said children in their visages and lineaments of their bodies to the said Blakeway."

Catherine apparently rejected her children. Samuel More boarded them with a tenant of his father's, then arranged to deliver them to John Carver and Robert

Cushman for transportation to America—the declaration said to Virginia. They would be sufficiently kept and maintained with meat, drink, apparel, lodging, and at the end of seven years they should have 50 acres of land apiece in the "country of Virginia."

The More children were temporarily quartered in the London home of Thomas Weston, head of the Adventurers, awaiting the *Mayflower's* departure.

(The story of the More children, including the possibility that they were of royal descent, is told in the *New England Historical and Genealogical Register*, vol. 124 (1970), page 85; and in vol. 114 (1960), page 163; also in *The Mayflower Quarterly*, vol. 38 (1972) No. 1, page 5.)

Many families, like the Brewsters, were split. William and Dorothy Bradford were leaving their only child behind for reasons that have never been explained. John Bradford was only six years old.

Carver and Cushman, still in England buying provisions for the journey, were anticipating the time when they would finally sail and they would be reunited with their wives. Carver was childless, but Cushman had a boy of ten and a second wife he had rarely seen since their marriage about three years earlier.

All of the family of Isaac Allerton, a tailor, planned to go—his pregnant wife and three little children. Two-year-old Mary Allerton was destined to be the last survivor of the *Mayflower* voyage. And Isaac himself, after the death of his first wife, was destined to be a son-in-law of William Brewster.

In late July of 1620, it was at last time to begin the journey.

William Brewster was still in hiding, and he probably slipped aboard the *Mayflower* either in London or in Southampton.

In Leyden, Mary Brewster and her children walked through the doors of the Robinsons' big house for the last church service they would attend there together.

Robinson in his message urged the departing members of his congregation to be ready to receive whatever further truth God might reveal to them. "For," he declared, "it is not possible the Christian world should come so lately out of such thick Antichristian darkness, and that the full perfection of knowledge should break forth at once."

He encouraged them to join with other "godly" ministers who might come to the New World, and to seek unity in the Christian church, rather than division.

And he urged them to try to "shake off" the name of Brownists.

Although William Brewster probably did not hear this sermon, it agreed completely with his own views, and he always attempted to follow the counsel in it. William Bradford and Edward Winslow wrote down excerpts from the sermon, so that they were available for instructing the children as they grew up. Both accounts were eventually printed, Bradford briefly in his history, Winslow at length in *Hypocrisie Unmasked*.[35]

After the service the women remaining in Leyden cooked a glorious farewell dinner in honor of those departing. Winslow called it a feast. These people knew that it was a last farewell for some, and a certain long separation for others. They wept and then consoled themselves in singing their familiar psalms. Many of the congregation were good singers, according to Winslow, who recalled the psalms that evening as "the sweetest melody that ever mine ears heard."[36]

At daybreak the next morning, July 21, 1620, Mary Brewster and the children boarded a canal boat for the journey to Delft Haven. It was probably moored in a canal just a few steps from their home. All the Brewster children went aboard, those who were staying in Holland as well as those who were going to America, so it was not yet a final parting. Most of the members of the church were going as far as Delft Haven, some twenty miles away. Some of their Amsterdam friends came too.

They watched the familiar scenes blur as the boat slid down the canal, past the water-gate where the canal left Leyden, through the pastures and beside the towns lining the canal between Leyden and Delft. The canal passed through the city of Delft, where the travellers could see the Old Kirk and the red-tiled roof of the house where William of Orange had been assassinated. Again the boat was gliding through pastures, or rather above them, for the canal was elevated there. Through the sluice gates the boat passed, and at last to the Delft Haven quai, where the *Speedwell* was waiting.[37]

The English wives who would remain in Leyden brought forth still another feast, which the travellers could remember longingly in the lean days ahead. John Robinson led his congregation in one last prayer, falling to his knees and they joining him. Again there were tears. "They accompanied us to the ship," Winslow said, "but were not able to speak one to another for the abundance of sorrow to part."[38]

The ship was ready to sail, the wind was fair. The moment had come. The *Speedwell* carried almost half the little English congregation aboard her, while the others on the quai strained to catch the final glances. At last, Jonathan Brewster and his sisters and the others remaining behind climbed aboard the canal boat returning to Leyden.

Aboard the *Speedwell*, Mary Brewster and her two young boys felt the winds of the English channel and smelled the salty spray as the ship headed for England.

Years later, William Bradford, telling of the departure, wrote the lines which still later gave the Pilgrims their name:

"So they left that goodly and pleasant city which had been their resting place near twelve years; but they knew they were pilgrims, and looked not much on those things, but lift up their eyes to the heavens, their dearest country, and quieted their spirits."[39]

Bradford was using the word "pilgrim" in the same sense it was used in the 11th book of the Epistle to the Hebrews in the Bible, which he cites—meaning a stranger, a traveller, a wanderer, one who seeks a country.

7   The Greatest Adventure Begins

T HE *SPEEDWELL'S* PASSENGERS saw the *May-flower's* tall masts rising in the harbor of South-ampton when the *Speedwell* arrived there after a spray-tossed but uneventful channel crossing. William Brewster joined his family there, and the passengers from Leyden met the newcomers.

Arguments with the Adventurers continued to the water's edge. Thomas Weston descended on Southampton long enough to demand that the colonists agree to the terms Cushman had agreed to. They refused absolutely and wrote a letter to the Adventurers, to set the record straight in writing. They also offered to extend their seven-year contract if the first seven years should not be profitable. Fortunately the Adventurers ignored the offer.

Weston refused to give them another penny. To meet the final pre-departure expenses, the hard-pressed colonists sold some of their supplies; they had a surplus of butter.

At last, the *Mayflower* and the *Speedwell* sailed out of the harbor bound for the New World. It was August 5, harvest time in England. The farmers in the land the settlers were leaving had already cut their hay. Apples and pears were ripening on the trees. By the time the ships could hope to reach New England, it would be autumn, and they would have no harvest in the new land.

The colonists had already taken the first steps toward civil government. Brewster was to be in charge of the church, the main concern of their migration, until Robinson could come. There had been a brief hope that an ordained minister would join the present voyage, but this had come to nothing.

The colony was not to be a theocracy, however. Brewster was always consulted on important civil decisions, but he never held any office in the colony's government.

Brewster probably read aloud to the congregation the letter which John Robinson sent them just before sailing. It was a final counsel for peace with each other. Robinson noted that they were about to become "a body politic." None of them were of special eminency, so they should choose persons who would promote the common good. And once chosen, these persons should receive "all due honour and obedience in their lawful administrations."[1]

The first officials chosen were Christopher Martin, one of the new members, and Robert Cushman. Martin was to be governor of the group in the *Mayflower* during the voyage, and Cushman governor in the *Speedwell.*

Martin turned out to be a martinet, and Cushman's health was failing.

The *Speedwell* started to leak a week after they left Southampton. Both ships had to turn about and sail for Dartmouth, where precious time and money were consumed in repairs.

Robert Cushman poured out his anguish in a letter sent while the ships were in the harbor at Dartmouth, addressed to his friend Edward Southworth in London.

Cushman was sick. "What to call it I know not, but it is a bundle of lead, as it were, crushing my heart more and more these fourteen days," he wrote. He lamented over the unseaworthy *Speedwell*—"as open and leaky as a sieve." The winds were fair, the colonists were losing valuable time and they were eating up the provisions they counted on for the first few months in America. The arrogant Governor Martin refused to account for the money he had spent on provisions and was performing like a dictator. "He so insulteth over our poor people, with such scorn and contempt, as if they were not good enough to wipe his shoes," Cushman wrote. Martin would not let the passengers go ashore "lest they should run away," and he had managed to offend the sailors.[2]

On August 23 the two ships sailed from Dartmouth. This time they had gone only a hundred leagues beyond the tip of England at Land's End when the *Speedwell* again began to leak. They anchored in the harbor at Plymouth, and this time the *Speedwell* was pronounced unfit for the Atlantic journey. Bradford believed that the ship's apparent troubles were caused deliberately by the master and his company in order to avoid the dangerous voyage and cancel their promise to stay a year in America.[3]

In Plymouth harbor, the *Speedwell* passengers carried their belongings off the ship and aboard the crowded *Mayflower*. This was again a time of parting though, because the *Mayflower* could not take all of the *Speedwell* passengers. About twenty remained in England. Robert Cushman and his family stayed behind, largely because of his declining health. Most of those who finally sailed were the youngest and strongest of the group.

At last, on September 6, the *Mayflower* sailed out of

the harbor of Plymouth and into the history of America.

Brewster was about 53 years old. Once again he was leaving an old life behind and beginning a new adventure, just as he had done when he left Scrooby for Cambridge University, and when he left Cambridge for the excitement of the service of the Elizabethan diplomat William Davison. Just as he had done when he rode back north from London to begin the quiet life serving the Scrooby post. Just as he had done when he fled from England to Holland. Now, at 53, he was leaving England and Holland behind, never to see them again. He would spend whatever remained of his life in the strange raw wilderness of America.

John Carver was about the same age as Brewster, and James Chilton, a tailor from Canterbury who had not been a member of the congregation, was 57 and the oldest of the passengers.

There were a few in their forties, but most of the adults were in their twenties or thirties. Of the 102 passengers, 32 were children, and three of the women were pregnant.

Before the ship sailed, Brewster knew only the passengers who had also been living in Leyden. There were 40 from Leyden and 39 freemen joined the ship in England. There were also five "hired hands" and 18 classed as servants.[4]

In the forced intimacy of the crowded *Mayflower*, they mingled. Gilbert Winslow, Edward Winslow's 20-year-old brother, had joined the ship in England. Just before it left Southampton, John Alden, a strong young man with blond hair, had been signed on as a "hired hand" to tend the barrels in which the precious supply of beer and fresh water was carried. He could stay in America or go back to England as he liked. The company hoped he would stay. As Bradford put it, Alden was "a hopeful young man."[5]

They nearly lost another strong young man, John Howland, when a wave swept him overboard during a storm. Howland was able to grab the topsail halyards as he went over the side and to keep his grasp even when he went under water. The crew hauled him up and fished him in with a boat hook.

Although the first part of the crossing went well, by mid-Atlantic the storms were so severe that the sailors had to shorten the sails and drift with the wind for many days. The passengers were ill and miserable, and thoughts of Blackwell's ill-fated voyage to Virginia would have hung heavy in their minds.

During the most severe storm of all, sea water began to leak through the boards, and one of the main beams cracked. The passengers offered the captain the use of a huge iron screw which they had brought along for possible construction purposes. The crew placed the great screw under the cracked beam and raised it into place, then put a post under it and completed the repairs. They caulked the leaks, Captain Christopher Jones pronounced the ship fit to continue the journey "if they did not overpress her with sails," and the *Mayflower* sailed on westward. The great iron screw that braced the beam may have come from Brewster's printing press, salvaged before the authorities who came to seize the type could seize it too.[6]

Relations between the passengers and the crew improved somewhat. They had gotten off to a bad start because of "Governor" Christopher Martin's arrogance in port. Once the ship was under way, Martin was less in evidence, possibly because of seasickness.

Still, crew-passenger relations on this cramped ship were edgy. One sailor was particularly offensive. Bradford writes that this crewman "would alway be contemning the poor people in their sickness and cursing them daily with grievous execrations; and did not let to tell them he hoped to help to cast half of them overboard before they came to their journey's end."

Instead, the offensive sailor was himself stricken by illness. He died, and his body was the first to be cast overboard for burial at sea. The Pilgrims regarded this as God's punishment. Said Bradford, "Thus his curses light on his own head, and it was an astonishment to all his fellows for they noted it to be the just hand of God upon him." The Pilgrims believed in a personal God, who would reward their right efforts, though sometimes grievously testing them, and who would punish those who persecuted their church.[7]

One passenger died, William Butten, aged 22, a servant of Samuel Fuller. Butten's home is listed as Austerfield, the birthplace of Bradford.[8] Clues like this, and the suggestion that some of those who joined the ship in England lived in nonconformist neighborhoods of London indicate that some of the people boarding the *Mayflower* in England may have had religious motives themselves for joining the expedition. Butten, like the sailor, was buried at sea.

Numerically, the passenger list was unchanged by his death. Elizabeth Hopkins' baby was born at sea and appropriately named Oceanus. The baby's father, Stephen, was the only passenger who had ever been in the New World. Almost certainly he was the Stephen Hopkins who sailed for Virginia aboard the ship *Sea Adventure* back in 1609. The Hopkins of the *Sea Adventure* was chosen by its chaplain to read the psalms and other Biblical passages during Sunday services. Before that ship could reach Virginia, it was wrecked without loss of life off the coast of the island of Bermuda. Sir George Somers, commander of the expedition, and Sir William Gates, who was en route to take up his duties as newly appointed Governor of Virginia, commanded the shipwrecked crew to build a small ship that would take the company on to Virginia. Some members of the crew rebelled against this order, fearing that if they reached Virginia in a small ship which was not strong enough to return to England, they might be forced to stay in Virginia and labor for the Adventurers. The rebels were charged with mutiny and several were executed. The chaplain's assistant, Stephen Hopkins, although a leader of the mutiny, was pardoned by the Governor when Hopkins pleaded that his wife and children would be ruined if he were not spared. The crew then built a small bark and proceeded to Virginia. Among the clues that Hopkins of the Bermuda mutiny and Hopkins of the *Mayflower* were the same man are these: Hopkins of the *Mayflower* was sent with the Pilgrims' first land exploring party to give "counsel and advice." He recognized an Indian trapping device and knew some Indian words. And in later years, he had several quasi-mutinous conflicts with Plymouth authorities.[9]

John Goodman, a Leyden linen-weaver, brought his dogs along, the only ones on the ship—a mastiff bitch and a small spaniel, sex unspecified.

In the cold of a November dawn, the ship's lookout spied the shore of Cape Cod. The passengers strained for a sight of this strange land as they came closer to the bluffs of Truro. They were "not a little joyful," Bradford writes with understatement. But the ship did not immediately anchor. Its officers and the passengers knew that this was the cape marked on John Smith's map. There has always been disagreement over the Pilgrims' plans—where they intended to settle. The only first hand account is Bradford's. He said that they were resolved "to find some place about Hudson's River for their habitation." The *Mayflower* did sail south, past the tip of Cape Cod, but after a few hours the ship's company found themselves in such dangerous waters that they were barely able to head about and return back up the coast. They kept to the open sea for the night, and on their second dawn in the New World they sailed past the tip of Cape Cod and anchored in a good, safe harbor.[10]

The voyage was over. Whatever lay ahead among the thick trees that grew then on that strange coast, the travelers had passed safely through the ocean's perils. Brewster led them in a prayer of gratitude as they fell upon their knees.

Despite their urgency to go ashore, the Pilgrim leaders insisted on assembling most of the men in the *Mayflower* cabin so that they would sign a document pledging that they would establish and support a civil government.

This was the famous Mayflower Compact. It was a promise, signed by most of the male passengers, that they would establish a "civil body politic" and abide by its laws. The Compact may have been written by Brewster, the only member of the company with knowledge of government documents. Or it may have been written by Bradford or another; all the colonists had experience in church government.

(The original Mayflower Compact has been lost. A copy first appeared in 1622 in *Mourt's Relation*, in an account apparently written by Bradford. The names of the signers appeared first in 1669 in Nathaniel Morton's *New England Memorial*.)

Bradford notes that one reason for drawing up the Compact and securing the signatures was that some of the people who joined the ship at London had been making "discontented and mutinous speeches." These malcontents said that they would do as they liked when they came ashore, because the Virginia Company had no authority in New England.[11] Was Stephen Hopkins stirring up another mutiny? At any rate, he signed the pact. Then, or subsequently, John Carver was named Governor.

And then, at last, at long last, it was time to send the first party ashore to explore this strange new land. Brewster at 53 stood on the deck and watched a party of the younger men climb over the side, row ashore in a small boat and disappear in the brush.

Bradford wrote later of the colonists' fears of this wild winter landscape, where there were no friends to welcome them nor inns to entertain them. Said Bradford, "Besides, what could they see but a hideous and desolate wilderness, full of wild beasts and wild men—and what multitudes there might be of them they knew not."[12]

The exploring party under Captain Standish brought some reassurance when they returned to the ship. They found sandy ground, much like the dunes of Holland which the Pilgrims had known, but much better. There was good black topsoil, a spade's depth. They found trees, oaks, pines, juniper and others, and they brought sweet-smelling juniper logs back to the *Mayflower* because they were running out of firewood. Best of all they saw no other persons and no sign of habitation.[13]

The next day was Sunday, and Brewster led his congregation in prayers of thankfulness for their deliverance from the perils of the ocean. The day was spent quietly aboard the *Mayflower*.

Monday morning Mary Brewster and the other women

of the *Mayflower* celebrated the first wash-day in the New
World. This must have been a jubilant landing, with an
armed party to guard them, and probably most of the
Mayflower passengers going too, anxious to walk this
new earth with their own feet. The women washed their
piles of clothes, probably in a fresh-water pond separated
from the sea by a narrow strip of sand on the coast
of what is now Provincetown. The pond has since dis-
appeared.[14]

The shallop which had been stored between decks on
the *Mayflower* was brought ashore for repairs of damage
caused in the battering of the ocean storms.

The children of the *Mayflower* romped on the beach
and relished a chance for a run on the sands. Some of
the Pilgrims picked up shellfish—clams, oysters and mus-
sels, which they ate and soon regretted.

Two days later a party of 16 men headed by Captain
Standish set out on an extensive exploration to determine
whether a settlement could be made in this area. Brewster was not a member of the party, but Bradford, a much
younger man, was. So was Stephen Hopkins, perhaps in
recognition of his earlier experience in America. The little army marched off single file into the cold November
wilderness, each carrying a musket and sword and wearing a corselet. They knew it might be a dangerous expedition, as did those remaining on board the *Mayflower*.

The explorers were gone for two days, but they all
returned safely with an account of their adventures.[15]
They had seen five or six Indians, whom they followed
but soon lost. They found springs of fresh water, which
they drank "with as much delight as ever we drunk drink
in all our lives." They saw deer and water fowl. Walking
up a little path, they discovered heaps of earth which
proved to be graves. They dug up a bow and other things

but replaced them in deference to the Indians "because we thought it would be odious unto them to ransack their sepulchers." Walking on, they found a place where a house had been, a kettle which had come from a European ship, and a buried basket full of this year's corn harvest. They carried some of the corn away in the kettle, determined to pay the Indians for the corn and to give them back the kettle if they should see them again.

The second night on the mainland was rainy; the men and their muskets were soaked as they marched through the forest. A sapling bent over next to a tree was an Indian deer trap, Stephen Hopkins, their authority on Indians, explained. William Bradford, coming up in the rear, stepped on the trap, which "gave a sudden jerk up, and he was immediately caught by the leg."

The men brought the corn back to the *Mayflower* to save it for planting. With the realization even then that they were making history, they called this expedition the "First Discovery."[16]

Explorers in other expeditions during the next few days ranged up and down Cape Cod in search of a settlement site, while they learned more of the area's animals and found further traces of its elusive inhabitants. The weather was cold, and while they sailed along the coast in their little boat, the spray froze on their clothes.

There was an encounter with the Indians. Early one morning, the Pilgrims of the exploring party heard "a great and strange cry," and one of the explorers who had been a short distance away came running to the others. "They are men, Indians, Indians!" he called. Arrows rained into the Pilgrim camp, and the Pilgrim men grabbed their muskets—the four of them that had them ready grabbed their muskets. Captain Standish fired a shot with his weapon, a "snaphance." The rest of the party within earshot on the beach by the shallop also fired their guns. The Indians shouted a battle cry.[17]

The Englishmen hoped that their musket shots would frighten the Indians away. The English were themselves frightened by the Indian arrows, which they managed to duck, and by the Indian cry, which sounded to them like "Woath woach ha ha hach woach." The Indians broke off the engagement and glided away into the woods.

The Pilgrims called the place "The First Encounter" and believed that "it pleased God to vanquish our enemies."[18]

At last, after ranging along the coast, and nearly losing the shallop and their lives in a stretch of rough sea, the explorers landed on the shores of a small island, happily uninhabited, built a fire despite the rain which had turned to snow and back to rain again. They had been searching for a harbor which their pilot, Robert Coffin, had remembered from an earlier voyage.

The next day was sunny, and the party spent the day resting on the island and drying out. They spent a second day on the island too, because that was Sunday, and returned to serious exploration Monday morning.

Early Monday, they sounded the harbor and determined that it was deep enough for ships. They sailed to the shore and explored it, where they found cornfields and little running brooks. It was "fit for situation," in Bradford's words. He adds, "At least it was the best they could find, and the season and their present necessity made them glad to accept of it."[19]

This was Plymouth harbor, named by Captain John Smith years earlier. It was sheer coincidence that the Pilgrim settlement bore the name of the English harbor of Plymouth from which the *Mayflower* had finally embarked.

Brewster watched the exploration party returning after six days with their glad discovery of a settlement site. He knew that he would have to break the news of the death of Bradford's wife to him. She had drowned five days earlier.

There have never been any details of the death of Dorothy May Bradford, aged 23, whether accidental or suicide. Probably no one knew. But somehow she slipped or fell over the side into the icy waters. Bradford himself never mentioned her death in his history. In a notebook in which he also recorded deaths of other settlers, Bradford wrote, "Dec. 7. Dorothy, Wife to Mr. William Bradford."[20]

With the decision to plant their colony in Plymouth, the Pilgrims ended their search for a home, 13 years after the Brewsters left Scrooby. The *Mayflower* sailed into its harbor and anchored a mile and a half off shore. By December 25 all the able-bodied male colonists rowed ashore to begin cutting down trees for a Common House to serve as a general shelter until they could build separate houses.

The Pilgrims did not celebrate Christmas; they reasoned that the celebration was not warranted by the scripture.

Desperately they worked each day as long as the light would last to build their Common House, admittedly a make-shift structure about 20-feet square, built of rough-hewn boards (not round logs), covered with woven branches and clay, known as wattle-and-daub construction, which provided some insulation. The roof was thatched. The building became a storehouse, a shelter for the party left each night as a guard, and within a few days it was a shelter for the sick and the dying.

The settlers had often been soaked with icy rain or sea

spray. They were exhausted by marches to explore the new land, by the physical effort of felling trees and building the shelter. One after another, they became sick, and many of them died.

Richard Britteridge, who had come aboard the *Mayflower* in London, died aboard ship shortly after it anchored off Plymouth. He was the first to be buried ashore.

Mary Allerton's baby was born dead, although Susanna White's baby had been delivered safely while the *Mayflower* was anchored off Cape Cod. He was appropriately named Peregrine, a wanderer or pilgrim, and he lived to the age of 83.

Christopher Martin, who had been responsible for much of the purchasing before the *Mayflower* sailed, was dying. He called Governor Carver to his bedside to pass on some information about the accounts.

Bradford was stricken ill, commencing with a violent pain in his hipbone. He eventually recovered, but others among the colonists were dying, sometimes one or two in a single day.

Only six or seven colonists escaped the general sickness. Brewster was one of them; Standish was another. Brewster and the Captain and the few others who were not ill cared for the sick and comforted the dying, and sadly buried the dead.

Bradford gratefully wrote later that they "spared no pains night nor day, but with abundance of toil and hazard of their own health, fetched them wood, made them fires, dressed them meat, made their beds, washed their loathsome clothes, clothed and unclothed them. In a word, did all the homely and necessary offices for them which dainty and queasy stomachs cannot endure to hear named; and all this willingly and cheerfully, without any grudging in the least, showing herein their true love unto their friends and brethren; a rare example and worthy to be remembered."[21]

Despite the illness, settlers able to do so went on with the business of building the two rows of houses close together that would make their town. And on Sunday, January 21, Brewster carried his Bible to the Common House and preached his first sermon on shore.

He had hoped to hold a service there a week earlier, but the thatched roof of the Common House caught fire early that Sunday morning. The house was packed with the sick, who arose from their beds to carry outside the gunpowder and muskets stored there before the sparks could reach them. Then they put out the fire, which had damaged only the thatch. The next day the roof was repaired.

Captain Standish mounted his cannons on a wooden platform on a steep hill overlooking the settlement and harbor beyond. Captain Standish's wife, Rose, died of the sickness.

A few weeks after the landing, Standish was formally elected, by popular vote, Captain-General, and given authority to command the little army which would defend Plymouth. He carried this responsibility until shortly before his death nearly forty years later.

In the new colony the deaths from the sickness continued: Mary Allerton, whose baby had been born dead a few weeks earlier, died too, leaving three young children. Edward Winslow, the printer apprentice in Brewster's Leyden publishing enterprise, lost his wife, Elizabeth. Eighteen-year-old Priscilla Mullins lost both parents and her brother. William White, father of Peregrine and of five-year-old Resolved, died. And on and on.

There was sickness among the *Mayflower* crew too, and the sailors burned juniper branches aboard to mask the odors of death.

By the end of March nearly half of the colony had died. The others, only about fifty by now, formed new households, expanding them to take in the remaining members of shattered families. Bradford was again living with the Brewsters.

Both William and Mary Brewster survived the sickness, as did nine-year-old Love and six-year-old Wrestling. Six-year-old Richard More, one of the two More children "put to" the Brewsters, lived, but the other child died. So did a brother living with the Carvers and a sister living with the Winslows.[22]

The survivors of the *Mayflower* crossing stood on shore to wave good-bye as the ship finally sailed for England April 5, 1621, carrying letters about the many losses. Despite the deaths, the colony was established. The ship delayed its return until April because of the wintry weather, because members of its crew were also taken sick, and because the Pilgrims needed the ship for living quarters while they were constructing their own.

The *Mayflower*'s Captain Christopher Jones had indeed been a help to his passengers in their need. He accompanied them on some of their explorations, sent beer to the sick when one of his crew refused to give it to them, and occasionally sent them game or fish.

The settlers wept when the *Mayflower*'s masts became thin lines on the horizon. But not one of them returned to England aboard her.

8 Life in the Flourishing Colony

N EARLY A YEAR after the *Mayflower* settlers had
first sailed past the tip of Cape Cod, one of their
Indian neighbors ran into the Pilgrim village with the
news that a ship had been sighted passing the cape and
headed for Plymouth.

Fearing that the vessel might be a French raider,
Captain Standish fired off a cannon to call his little army
in from their fishing or their fields. However as the ship
came into harbor, the British colors were flying. Over-
joyed, the settlers watched a small boat coming ashore
while the 55-ton ship *Fortune* rode at anchor. The *Fortune*
was bringing new settlers.

One of the arrivals was Jonathan Brewster, the oldest
son of William and Mary Brewster. Still a widower,
Jonathan, now 28 years old, had left his trade as a Leyden
ribbon maker to settle in this rude New World. There
was so much to say to each other in these first few
hours—news of Jonathan's sisters, Fear and Patience,
still in Leyden, and of the Robinsons and others. In return, Jonathan heard a report on the colony's development since the *Mayflower's* departure six months earlier.

Seven other men from the Leyden church and the
wives of two of them also came as settlers. Robert

Cushman, the Pilgrims' agent in England who had been ill and stayed behind with the *Speedwell* a year earlier, had recovered from his sickness to sail on the *Fortune*. He was still working on the agreement between the settlers and Adventurers and planned to return to England when the *Fortune* returned. He expected to settle in Plymouth eventually though. Cushman's 14-year-old son, Thomas, accompanied him and remained in Plymouth.

The Adventurers also sent 17 men, one woman and five children. John Winslow, another of Edward and Gilbert Winslow's brothers, came to join them. Another passenger, Thomas Prence, a 21-year-old carriage maker, eventually became William Brewster's son-in-law and Governor of Plymouth. Many of the new arrivals sent by the Adventurers brought little with them in the way of food, bedding, or other essentials, but somehow the Pilgrims absorbed them, finding room for all in their crowded homes.[1]

Brewster, showing his eldest son the comforts of their hand-wrought home, knew that the Pilgrim village was still a precarious undertaking—but it was a village now where there had been empty fields and forest only a year earlier.

Jonathan saw the Common House, the platform on the hill where Standish mounted his brass cannons, three storage buildings, and the seven small individual houses. Each had a fireplace of sorts, with a chimney of wood plastered over with clay, used both for warmth and for cooking. The houses were dark, since windows would let in more cold. There was no glass, but some light came in the little windows through heavy paper soaked in linseed oil. The floors were earthen, but families could cut rushes to spread over them if they liked. The steep roof was thatched, and there was a loft where the children could sleep. Accidental fire was a constant danger.[2]

The government set up as provided by the Mayflower Compact was in good order. Brewster was always consulted on "weighty matters" by the Governor, now William Bradford. Bradford had been elected the previous spring after Governor Carver, returning from the fields, collapsed and died. Isaac Allerton, who had been a tailor in Leyden, was elected Assistant Governor.

Relations with the Indians were amazingly good.

The Pilgrims had unknowingly chosen a site where an Indian village stood about four years earlier and had been abandoned. The tribe who lived there had been wiped out by smallpox, so there were no native claims on the territory.

During the early weeks in Plymouth, the settlers uneasily noted Indians "skulking about," but the first contact was with a tall Indian man who strode into town, nearly naked, and approached a group of startled Pilgrims. "Welcome," he said in English, and asked for beer.[3]

This was Samoset, chief of a tribe in the Maine region, who had dealt with English traders. Samoset in turn brought Squanto, who became what the Pilgrims called a special instrument sent of God for their good.

Squanto was the only survivor of the tribe which once inhabited Plymouth. A year or two before the plague struck his tribe, Squanto was kidnapped by an English sea captain and sold as a slave in Spain. Somehow he found his way to London, where he lived with a merchant and learned English. A few months before the *Mayflower* left England, Squanto sailed for New England aboard another English vessel. Squanto found that his family and his entire tribe had died in the epidemic, and he lived for a time with another tribe, the Wampanoag.

Squanto preferred the English way of life, and he soon moved in with the Pilgrims, attaching himself particularly to Bradford. His knowledge of Indian language and customs was invaluable to the Pilgrims. Through Squanto and Samoset they met the Wampanoag and the tribe's powerful Chief Massasoit. Massasoit and his braves visited Plymouth, where they agreed to a treaty of peace proposed by the Pilgrims. These were the terms of the treaty:

1. That neither he [Massasoit] nor any of his should injure or do hurt to any of their people.

2. That if any of his did hurt to any of theirs, he should send the offender, that they might punish him.

3. That if anything were taken away from any of theirs, he should cause it to be restored; and they should do the like to his.

4. If any did unjustly war against him, they would aid him; if any did war against them, he should aid them.

5. He should send to his neighbours confederates to certify them of this, that they might not wrong them, but might be likewise comprised in the conditions of peace.

6. That when their men came to them, they should leave their bows and arrows behind them.[4]

The drafter of the treaty may well have been Brewster, based on memories of the English-Dutch treaty on which Davison worked in the service of Queen Elizabeth. The treaty with Massasoit endured and in the main was observed by both sides until after Massasoit's death about forty years later.

By November 1621, when the *Fortune* landed, the Pilgrims had succeeded well enough with their farming, fishing and hunting to feed themselves, though not lavishly, and occasionally to entertain the Indians, who apparently had even less to eat than they did. Ninety Indians attended the first Thanksgiving feast shortly before the arrival of the *Fortune*. The Indians contributed five deer to it.

While Jonathan was still in Leyden, he knew of the many deaths of the first Plymouth winter, among them several young married people of his own generation. Arriving in Plymouth, he learned that the widower Edward Winslow had married the widow Susanna White in May, the first marriage in the colony. Bradford as Governor performed the marriage. The Pilgrims considered marriage a civil contract, not a religious ceremony.

Jonathan Brewster realized that the colony's leadership had passed to his own generation. His parents were now the oldest people in the colony, although they were still in their early fifties.

The meeting house was overflowing on the first Sunday after the arrival of the *Fortune*. All the people of Plymouth were required to attend church services, whether or not they belonged to the church. Before Robert Cushman returned to London aboard the *Fortune*, he preached a sermon at one of the Sunday services. Ironically, this is the only early Plymouth sermon to survive; it was published in London in 1622. Cushman, a deacon of the church, urged the Pilgrims to work for each other's good. Some of the new settlers were anxious to break their bonds with the Adventurers and strike out on their own. Cushman knew that the colony could not survive without the help of the Adventurers, unsatisfactory and uncertain as it was.[5]

Not one of Brewster's sermons survived, although for years he preached twice every Sunday, powerfully and profitably, Bradford said. He had the respect and affection of his listeners; they heeded his admonitions and many who had not been members in the early days joined the church. He realized that people forced to stand with heads bowed for lengthy public prayers would find their attention flagging, so he led them in shorter, more frequent prayers.[6]

Jonathan Brewster settled into the life at Plymouth—the constant building of homes to house the newcomers, building of a palisade around the whole community, building a new Common House on the hill which would serve as both meeting house and fort, anxiety as the colony faced semi-starvation between one harvest and the next.

Ships called occasionally, bringing letters with news from England. King James had dissolved Parliament in anger. The Lord Chancellor Francis Bacon had been dismissed from his post and found guilty of accepting bribes from persons involved in law suits. Bacon was fined and sentenced to the Tower "during the King's pleasure." How familiar the wording of the sentence was to William Brewster, reminiscent of the sentence handed down to Davison after the death of Mary Queen of Scots.

Aboard one of the ships in 1622 was an English passenger, John Pory, a man in his fifties, who was a welcome guest of the Brewsters and Bradford. A sophisticated traveler, Pory was a Cambridge graduate who had once served in the House of Commons, and spent some years in Virginia as secretary-recorder of that colony. He was the first speaker of the Virginia Assembly. However, Sir Edwin Sandys, Brewster's friend in the Virginia Company, had accused Pory of enriching himself at the colonists' and the company's expense. Pory was on his way back to England somewhat in disgrace, but he was nevertheless most welcome in Plymouth.

Brewster and his guest may have reminisced about the days when Brewster was printing "seditious" books in Leyden and British Ambassador Sir Dudley Carleton was trying to hunt him down. Pory was a good friend of Carleton's. And there were those same books, some of them, kept as treasures in Brewster's rough-hewn cabin on the edge of the wilderness. Brewster and Bradford gave Pory a few books—they had several copies of some of them—to read on the long voyage back to England.

He wrote a letter of thanks to Bradford and Brewster, specifically mentioning books by Pastor Robinson and Harry Ainsworth. Pory wrote: "And what good (who knows) it may please God to work by them, through my hands (though most unworthy), who finds such high content in them."

After Pory returned to England, he wrote a long letter to the Virginia Company's head, the Earl of Southampton, praising the Pilgrims and their industry. However short of food they were from time to time, they had feasted Pory with blue fish, lobster and grapes.[7]

Peace with Massasoit and his Wampanoag tribe continued, but in 1623 the Pilgrims had a brief and bloody clash with another tribe, the Massachusetts. They had heard that the Massachusetts were planning to attack Plymouth and another recently established English settlement, Wessagusset.

Captain Standish commanded the expedition, heading a party of eight who lured the Indian leaders into a Wessagusset cabin, barred the door, and killed three Indians in hand-to-hand fighting. Four others were killed moments later either by the Standish party or by the Wessagusset settlers. Standish cut off the head of Witu-wamet, one of the slain Indians, and carried the bloody trophy back to Plymouth. Wituwamet had once insulted the fiery English captain.

Clearly the Pilgrim community had no immediate sense of guilt over the slayings. They set up the head of Witu-wamet above their fort, as they had seen so many sev-ered heads of the King's enemies impaled in London. It remained there for years, a bleached skull.

John Robinson, though in Leyden, was still their pas-tor, and he wrote a strong letter of reproach, addressing it to Bradford as the Governor responsible for the colo-ny's action. Bradford includes the entire letter in his his-tory and enters no defense.[8]

"Concerning the killing of those poor Indians," Robin-son brought up the subject of the slaughter and discussed it at length. "Oh, how happy a thing it had been," he lamented, "if you had converted some before you had killed any!" (In this sentence, "before" is surely used in the sense of "rather than.") Conversion of the Indians had been one of the Pilgrims' original stated aims.

Robinson pointed out that the Pilgrims were "no mag-istrates" over the Indians. He advised Bradford to re-strain Standish, in whose character "there may be want-ing that tenderness of the life of man (made after God's image) which is meet."

Robinson's letter did not reach Bradford until the spring of 1624, almost a year after the Indians were killed.

Robinson's admonitions were undoubtedly repeated in Brewster's sermons to the little colony. Personal criti-cism was regarded as proper, coming from the pastor or the elder. Many years later, after Brewster's death, Bradford wrote of Brewster, "In teaching, he was very moving and stirring of affections, also very plain and distinct in what he taught; by which means he became the more profitable to the hearers. He had a singular good gift in prayer, both public and private, in ripping up the heart and conscience before God in the humble confession of sin, and begging the mercies of God in Christ for the pardon of the same."[9]

The Pilgrims heeded Pastor Robinson's rebuke. There were no more preemptive strikes. Bradford's only comment on Robinson's letter was that it expressed the tender love and care of a true pastor over the people.[10]

A few months after the Indians were killed, in the summer of 1623 the Plymouth settlers were looking forward to the arrival of two ships carrying 93 more settlers and some badly needed provisions. Aboard one ship, the *Anne*, were both of the Brewster daughters, Patience, now 23, and Fear, now 17. They had been with the Robinsons in Leyden.

Governor Bradford was awaiting the arrival of a bride. Some time during the three years since the *Mayflower* left England, Edward Southworth died in London, leaving his wife Alice and two young children. Edward and Alice Southworth had been members of the Leyden church, and were married a few months before William Bradford married Dorothy May. Now Bradford had written to Alice proposing marriage, and she accepted.

Captain Standish, a widower since the first winter, was also expecting a bride to whom he had proposed by mail. Her first name was Barbara, her last is unknown now, and tradition reports that she was a sister of Standish's first wife.

Many of the other Pilgrims were awaiting family

members and friends. The happy expectation turned into anxiety when it appeared that the ship might have been lost at sea.

Late in June, the master of the English ship *Plantation*, calling at Plymouth, told Bradford that the men of the *Plantation* had sighted another English ship at sea some days earlier. Sailing alongside, some of the sailors of the *Plantation* climbed aboard the other ship, the *Anne*, and learned that it was bound for Plymouth with many passengers. The two ships kept each other in sight for a time, but lost contact during a storm. There was a smaller ship also bound for Plymouth, the *Little James*, but the *Anne* had already lost contact with it. The people of Plymouth feared that the ships, like so many others travelling the dangerous Atlantic, might have gone down in the storm. They remembered the frightening sound of the *Mayflower's* beam cracking during their own crossing.

From Fort hill at Plymouth, the settlers scanned the eastern horizon, encouraged to hope by the *Plantation's* news that the two ships were on the way, yet in fear that they might never arrive.

At last, 14 agonizing days later, someone sighted the *Anne* far out in the bay, and everyone lined the shore for the first glimpse of a beloved face, wondering, "Has he changed? Has she changed? Have I changed?" It was nearly three years since the *Speedwell* had left Leyden.

The people waiting on shore were thin. They had been working even harder in America than they had worked in Leyden, and their faces were worn. Their clothing was worn ragged in some cases. But the families from Leyden knew of the hardships, rejoiced to see their dear ones, and looked forward to better days now that they were reunited.

Something of the yearning of these separated families appears in a letter written a few months later to William Brewster by Pastor Robinson when he learned of the Brewster daughters' safe arrival. Robinson wrote, "That which I most desired of God in regard of you, namely the continuance of your life and health, and the safe coming of these sent unto you; that I most gladly hear of, and praise God for the same. And I hope Mrs. Brewster's weak and decayed state of body will have some repairing by the coming of her daughters, and the provisions in this and former ships I hear is made for you."[11]

Mary Brewster's health was failing, although she was to live several years longer.

It was a joyous reunion, and the newcomers were entertained with fish, lobster, and a cup of spring water. There was no bread, no beer, and the Pilgrims never considered lobster a delicacy. However they reflected cheerfully that "man liveth not by bread only," and delighted in each other's company.

The welcome was repeated about ten days later when the smaller ship bound for Plymouth finally sailed into the harbor. This was the *Little James*, which was to remain for the settlers' use as a fishing and trading vessel.

Among the passengers on the two boats were many strangers sent by the Adventurers. Robert Cushman in an accompanying letter apologized, "It grieveth me to see so weak a company sent you; and yet had I not been here they had been weaker." There were also ten people who had come "on their particular," not allied economically to the Plymouth colony but subject to its government. Jonathan Brewster was to find a new wife in this group.

The last of the Scrooby congregation to make the long pilgrimage through Leyden to Plymouth was George

Morton, who arrived on the *Anne* along with his wife and four children. Mrs. Morton, the former Juliana Carpenter, was the sister of Alice Carpenter Southworth, who had come over to marry William Bradford.[12]

Bradford and Alice Southworth were married a few days after her arrival. The colony feasted with them on roast venison and "other such good cheer in such quantity that I could wish you some of our share," one of the guests wrote to his brother in England. The writer was Emmanuel Altham, a member of the Adventurers who had arrived on the *Little James*. Massasoit and some of the other Indians were also invited to the wedding feast. Massasoit, wearing a black wolf skin over his shoulder, strode up to the Governor's house accompanied by one of his five wives, four other tribal leaders, and more than 100 Indians with bows and arrows. Massasoit contributed three or four bucks and a turkey. The Pilgrims combined hospitality with a military display—a sort of troop review exercise and musket shooting. The Indians left their bows and arrows in the Governor's house, doubtless at the settlers' insistence, and entertained the wedding guests with some of their dancing.[13]

By the end of 1623, the colony was firmly established. Most of those from the Leyden church who could ever come were now in Plymouth. Twenty houses had been constructed in two lines with a street between them leading up the hill to the combination Common House and Fort at the top. Four or five of the houses were "very fair and pleasant," Altham reported. He added that "the rest (as time will serve) shall be made better." The settlers owned six goats, about fifty hogs and pigs and a number of hens.[14]

The returning ship *Anne* was loaded with clapboard and beaver, which reached its destination as many other ships did not. The 1623 harvest was plentiful, and Bradford wrote of the settlers years later in his history, "any general want or famine hath not been amongst them since to this day."[15]

The settlers' troubles continued for many years, especially wrangling with their greedy London creditors, but the colony was never in danger of failure.

Jonathan Brewster, whose first wife and a baby died in Leyden, married again on April 10, 1624. Her name was Lucretia Oldham, and she eventually bore him eight children, all recorded in the family notebook.[16]

On August 5, 1624, Jonathan's sister Patience married Thomas Prence, who had arrived in the *Fortune*. This was the ninth marriage at New Plymouth, William Bradford jotted down in his pocket notebook.[17]

All the while Jonathan was courting Lucretia and during the early years of their marriage, John Oldham, probably Lucretia's older brother, or possibly her uncle, was involved in one battle after another with the Pilgrim leaders and in fact with nearly everyone else he encountered. Bradford called Oldham malicious.

John Oldham was apparently not Lucretia's father. A 1600 baptismal record from Derby, England, cites the baptism of Lucretia, daughter of William Ouldham.[18]

However Lucretia accompanied John Oldham and his wife, also named Lucretia, and a child named Christian to Plymouth in 1623.

Oldham was the leader of some ten persons who arrived in the *Anne-Little James* migration "on their particular." The Adventurers had sent them to settle in Plymouth, subject to its government and obligated only to military service and payment of a yearly bushel of corn as tax. They were forbidden to trade with the Indians. They had no share in the joint stock, and no obligations toward the colony's debt. It was a bad arrangement, and it turned out badly.

Oldham's story is known almost entirely from the Pilgrims' Bradford history. Doubtless Oldham viewed it differently.[19]

As Bradford tells it, Oldham spent his first months in Plymouth stirring up trouble, inciting some of the non-church members to support him, and sending letters of complaint back to London by any ship passing. In the spring he had a strong confederate, an Anglican minister, John Lyford.

Since the days when the Plymouth colony was still a vision, the planners expected to bring Pastor John Robinson to join them within a short time. Repeatedly a controlling faction of the Adverturers prevented Robinson from coming. Robinson's presence in the colony would set the final seal of "Brownism" on it, in their opinion.

The ship that brought Lyford to Plymouth in March 1624 also brought a letter from Robinson to Brewster. Robinson wrote of the "deferring of our desired transportation—which I call desired rather than hoped for, whatsoever you are borne in hand by any others."[20]

By now there was really no hope, no expectation that he would ever come.

Instead the Adventurers sent Lyford. Robert Cushman wrote, "The preacher we have sent is (we hope) an honest plain man, though none of the most eminent and rare." Cushman had agreed reluctantly to the Adventurers' decision to send Lyford, but made it plain that he would not be considered pastor of the church unless the members chose him to be.[21]

Nevertheless as Lyford came ashore, cringing, weeping and bowing with a great show of humility, he was welcomed by the Pilgrims. He and his long-suffering wife

Sarah and their brood of children were given a house, entertained generously, and Lyford was invited to sit with Bradford's advisory council.

Lyford joined the church, recanting his former allegiance to the Established Anglican Church.

At about this time, John Oldham suddenly declared that he saw the error of his ways in stirring up trouble. His apology was accepted, and for a time "all things seemed to go very comfortably," in Bradford's words.[22]

However Oldham and Lyford were soon thick in conspiracy. One of their aims was what the Pilgrims most dreaded: setting up an Anglican Church in Plymouth.

The two conspirators were observed busy with much letter writing—letters destined for the next ship bound for England. Lyford was making remarks to adherents which "made them laugh in their sleeves," Bradford said.

Bradford and the other leaders feared that Lyford's and Oldham's letters might endanger the colony's safety. Bradford determined to see what was in those letters. Letter interception seems to have been a common practice; there were many references to it. At any rate, Bradford had no scruples in this regard; furthermore, he shortly discovered that Lyford himself had opened some of the colonists' letters.

Late one afternoon, when the ship *Charity* was preparing to sail for England, Bradford and a few others rowed out to the ship in a shallop and demanded all of Lyford's and Oldham's letters. The ship's master William Peirce complied. Bradford and his men sat down in the ship's cabin and started reading the letters. Oldham's penmanship was bad—scarcely legible—and anyway he had only written a few letters. But Lyford's handwriting was legible, and his intentions were scurrilous, in the

Pilgrims' view. They set to work making copies of most of the Lyford letters, keeping some of the originals and sending copies of them on to England.

The only letters that Bradford did not send to England were copies that Lyford himself had made of letters sent to William Brewster by an English friend and another written by Edward Winslow while he was in England, addressed to John Robinson in Holland. Lyford had come across these letters during the journey from England, opened them, and copied their contents to send back to his backers in England. Lyford had written his own acid comments in the margins of the letters he copied.

It was dark by the time Bradford and the others finished their copying. The shallop rowed back to Plymouth, and the *Charity* soon headed out to sea.

The conspirators saw the shallop's journey, but concluded that Bradford had decided to send some last-minute mail.

Bradford and his advisors said nothing for the moment. They wanted to "let things ripen" and find out how many were involved in the conspiracy.

The conspirators, Bradford said, were as brisk as ever. Growing bolder, Lyford and Oldham started picking quarrels with the other settlers. At last Oldham went too far. He insulted Captain Standish. Standish ordered him to stand watch just as other men took turns in doing. Oldham refused. He called Captain Standish a rascal, a beggarly rascal, and drew his knife. Other settlers heard the uproar and came running, and Oldham stormed at them. He called them traitors and rebels. Bradford said Oldham used "such foul language as I am ashamed to remember."

The settlers disarmed Oldham and shut him up in the fort until "he came to himself."

Insulting the Captain was dangerous; Wituwamet had

insulted the Captain and was slain. But the one action
the community absolutely would not tolerate was an
attempt to undermine its church. Lyford and Oldham
made this mistake one Sabbath. They held an Anglican
service for as many as wished to attend. In their intercepted letters they had confided plans for a "reformation
in church and commonwealth."

True, the Scrooby congregation had been founded in
just this fashion. But the Pilgrims had no intention of
granting religious toleration in Plymouth. They had sacrificed too much in establishing a sanctuary there for
their own persecuted church. Nevertheless, they did co-
operate with Anglican settlements located far enough
away that they were not considered a danger.

The conspiracy had ripened, and now Bradford showed
his hand, determined to prevent further mischief. He
called a court into session and charged Lyford and Oldham "with such things as they were guilty of" in the
presence of all the other settlers.

Lyford and Oldham denied the charges and demanded
proof. Bradford brought out the letters he had intercepted and in a moment of high drama read some of them
out in court. The letters were full of complaints about
the settlers, accusing them of unfair distribution of food,
of wasting tools and of working against the Adventurers.
Lyford recommended that another military captain be
sent to displace Standish, "for this Captain Standish
looks like a silly boy and is in utter contempt."

Oldham upbraided Bradford, furious that his letters
had been intercepted. He turned to his own supporters
among the settlers with the appeal, "My masters, where
is your hearts? Now show your courage, you have oft
complained to me so and so. Now is the time, if you will
do anything, I will stand by you."

He looked from face to face in the crowded meeting

house. Some of these men had complained to him, fawned on him. Not a man spoke. Oldham stood alone in his defiance.

Bradford turned to Lyford and asked if Lyford thought Bradford had done evil in opening the letters. Lyford was silent. He knew that if he accused Bradford of evil, he could himself be accused of the same evil, since he too had intercepted letters.

Bradford told the company of the letters Lyford had intercepted, that he "had dealt treacherously with his friends that trusted him, and stole their letters and opened them, and sent copies of them, with disgraceful annotations, to his friends in England." Bradford justified his own actions in opening letters by saying he did it as a magistrate, to prevent the mischief and ruin that the conspiracy would bring on the colony.

Both men were convicted.

Lyford burst into tears, crying that "his sins were so great that he doubted God would not pardon them, he was unsavory salt." He confessed that he had so wronged the settlers as "he could never make them amends."

Oldham was apparently unrepentant, so he received the harsher sentence.

Both men were ordered expelled from Plymouth. Lyford, in recognition of his tearful confession, was permitted to stay another six months. If he proved truly repentant, he might be entirely forgiven.

Oldham was banished immediately, although it was winter. His wife and family, who had been charged with nothing, were permitted to stay until he could provide a safe and comfortable move for them.

Oldham headed north. Some of the other malcontents from Plymouth who had not dared to speak in court went with him. They established a settlement about thirty miles away called Nantasket. During the next year Jonathan Brewster courted and married Lucretia. It may have been some time before Oldham's family joined him. Also Jonathan spent most of his life as an Indian trader, and Nantasket was a reasonable journey.

Lyford followed his tearful court confession with a fulsome public confession in church. He said that his sins were the result of pride, vain-glory and self-love. The leaders accepted his repentance, some of them with misgivings, and permitted him to resume teaching (preaching) in the church.

By August he was writing again secretly to the Adventurers with complaints about the Pilgrims. This letter, like the earlier ones, fell into Pilgrim hands. In it he protested to the Adventurers that everything in his earlier letters was true. Furthermore, he charged that many settlers were "destitute of the means of salvation." Lyford complained that "they have had no ministry here since they came, but such as may be performed by any of you by their own position, whatsoever great pretences they make. But herein they equivocate, as in many other things they do." He also complained that the settlers had changed his wages "ten times."

Bradford wrote to the Adventurers that the colonists had never agreed with Lyford to any wages at all, and that they knew of no bargain on the part of the Adventurers. "You sent him over to teach amongst us, and desired he might be kindly used; and more than this we know not. That he hath been kindly used, and far better than he deserves from us, he shall be judged first of his own mouth."

Bradford vigorously denied Lyford's attacks on the church:

"Next, he saith, they have had no ministry since they came, whatsoever pretenses they make, etc. We answer, the more is our wrong, that our Pastor is kept from us by these men's means, and then reproach us for it when they have done. Yet have we not been wholly destitute of the means of salvation as this man would make the world believe. For our reverend Elder [Brewster] hath laboured diligently in dispensing the Word of God to us, before he came; and since, hath taken equal pains with himself, in preaching the same. And, be it spoken without ostentation, he is not inferior to Mr. Lyford (and some of his betters) either in gifts or learning, though he would never be persuaded to take higher office upon him."

In the wake of the controversy, many who had not joined the Pilgrim church now did so. Bradford concluded that the troubles were a work of God, "to draw on men by unlikely means."

The spring of 1625 brought a return of the unruly Oldham. Oldham never feigned repentance. Any reproofs were "but as oil to the fire," Bradford wrote. Oldham boldy condemned them all as rebels and traitors.

Again they shut him up in the fort "till he was tamer."

When he was considered tame enough to leave the fort, he was forced to pass down the street between two rows of men with muskets. Each man gave him a thump on the breech with the butt end of his musket. At the beach, a small boat was waiting. Oldham was ordered into the boat and commanded to leave and "mend his manners."[24]

Thus Jonathan Brewster's in-law was banished a second time.

In the middle of this excitement, Edward Winslow

landed at Plymouth from his latest trip to England. In fact, the Pilgrims were so busy thumping Oldham that they did not even notice the arrival of the ship that brought Winslow.

Winslow walked ashore with the ship master William Peirce (the same captain who let Bradford copy the Old-ham-Lyford letters). Both men urged the Pilgrims not to spare either Oldham or Lyford. They had brought shocking new information about Lyford.

The Adventurers in England had disagreed: Should they believe Lyford's accusations against the settlers or the settlers' accusations against him? A meeting to hear the case was set, with two prominent men appointed as moderators.

Investigations into Lyford's background disclosed that while in charge of a parish in Ireland he seduced a young unmarried woman, one of his parishioners. For this, he had been forced to leave Ireland. This sorry spectacle out of Lyford's past persuaded the moderators that he was unfit for the ministry, regardless of his pretences of repentance.

The Pilgrims told Winslow and Peirce that the story confirmed what Mrs. Lyford had already told them. Overcome with grief and sorrow, she confided that before her marriage, Lyford had fathered a child by another woman. Furthermore, she contended, after the marriage he was always meddling with their servant maids.

Bradford sympathetically referred to Sarah Lyford as "a grave matron and of good carriage."[25]

With no further support from England, Lyford was finally forced to leave Plymouth. (He joined Oldham at Nantasket, later went to English settlements at Naumkeag, which later became Salem, and Gloucester Harbor. Still later, he was an Anglican pastor in Virginia,

where he died. His long-suffering widow returned to
Massachusetts and married Edmund Hobart of Hing-
ham.)[26]

Once again, William Brewster and his deacons had the
sole responsibility for the Pilgrim church. How they
yearned for John Robinson! But John Robinson died in
March of 1625, although his flock in Plymouth did not
learn of it for more than a year. He was buried under
the pavement in the main aisle of St. Peter's, across from
the home where he lived and preached. The Dutch had
great respect for Robinson.

Captain Standish, who had been in England on business for the Pilgrims, brought them the sad news of Robinson's death, and a letter from Mrs. Robinson's brother,
Roger White. The letter brought some comfort; the illness had been brief and there had been no pain. Robinson
had faithfully finished his course.

White also wrote of the deaths of England's King
James and Holland's Prince Maurice. So now Charles I
sat on the throne of England. White said there was great
hope of him, but he proved no more tolerant toward non-
conformist worship in England than his father had been.
White referred to Holland's late prince as "the old
prince, Grave Maurice." Brewster remembered him as
the young Prince Maurice, watching the splendid Earl of
Leicester arrive to defend Holland.[27]

By now Brewster himself was the "Grave Elder" that
tradition remembers.

His second daughter, Fear, was married to Isaac Allerton, a *Mayflower* passenger who had been a widower
since the death of his wife Mary that dreadful first
winter. The date of Fear's marriage is unknown, but it

must have been before 1627, when she is listed as Allerton's wife in a document dividing cattle among the settlers. Allerton was about twice Fear's age and the father of three half-grown children. He was a respected leader of the colony, an Assistant Governor, and was a long-time member of the Leyden church.[28]

Probably not long after he married Fear, Allerton sailed for London to continue negotiations with the Adventurers. Edward Winslow and Captain Standish performed similar missions in previous years. In the spring of 1627 Allerton returned to Plymouth; the colonists were satisfied with his work and sent him back to London again later that year.

Two chilling developments in England pointed up the dangers that nonconformists there still faced. Thomas Brewer, once Brewster's financial backer in the Leyden printing enterprise, had returned to England to live and was active in the Separatist cause. In 1626 he was imprisoned, charged with encouraging others to preach against the Church of England, and labeled "a perfect Brownist." He remained in prison until 1640.[29]

A Scottish minister, Alexander Leighton, was severely punished for publishing in the Netherlands in 1628 a book attacking the English church. He was sentenced to a fine of 100,000 pounds, to have his ears sliced off and his nose slit, to be branded on the face with the letters S.S. (for sower of sedition), and to be imprisoned for life. He was released after 11 years in the Fleet prison. Brewster added Leighton's "seditious" book to his library in Plymouth.[30]

By 1627, the little colony had grown to a population of 156 freemen and 20 or 30 indentured servants.

Brewster's house was located on a corner mid-way up the hill where the street leading up to the Common House was intersected by another street.[31]

In the intersection, a palisade of vertical planks surrounded artillery weapons placed to repel any attack.

Diagonally across from the Brewster house was the home of William Bradford and his growing family. John, the son Bradford left behind in Leyden, finally came to Plymouth in 1627. Alice Bradford's sons by her first marriage, Constant and Thomas, joined the family a year later. Robert Cushman's son, Thomas, was living with the Bradfords too. So were Alice's nephew, Nathaniel Morton, and two boys who had come over on the *Mayflower*. By now William and Alice Bradford had two children of their own; a third was born later. It was quite a household.[32]

When Brewster stepped outside his own front door, he could see the home of his son, Jonathan, next door on his right, and just beyond that, the home of his daughter, Patience, and her husband, Thomas Prence. On his left, two houses beyond the cross street, was the home of his other daughter, Fear, and Isaac Allerton. The two youngest Brewster boys, Love and Wrestling, were still at home.

For a little while, the Brewsters enjoyed the pleasure of their united family and the close community for which they had yearned.

On April 17, 1627 Mary Brewster died. Her health had been poor for some time.[33]

Brewster continued his duties as elder of the church. He did not administer the sacraments—baptism and communion—because he was not an ordained minister. The people had once urged him to write to John Robinson asking if the elder could not do this, since they had no ordained minister. Robinson replied firmly that it would not be lawful. But in other respects Brewster performed the minister's duties. He accepted Robinson's ruling without question. Brewster was modest, and, Bradford said, undervalued himself and his own abilities, while sometimes overvaluing others'.

About this time, an official of the Dutch colony at New Netherland paid a visit to Plymouth. Isaack De Rasieres wrote a letter describing his visit, which is one of the few eye-witness descriptions of the early Plymouth colony written by an outsider.[34]

The Pilgrims, with grateful memory of their kind treatment in Holland, welcomed him happily, sending a small boat to fetch him when he arrived at Aptucxet some twenty miles away. Once again those who had lived in Holland were talking away in Dutch with their visitor, pointing out all the landmarks of their little settlement, describing how they planted their corn.

De Rasieres was suitably impressed. "The houses," he wrote later, "are constructed of hewn planks, with gardens also enclosed behind and at the sides with hewn planks, so that their houses and courtyards are arranged in very good order, with a stockade against a sudden attack; and at the ends of the streets there are three wooden gates."

De Rasieres stayed for several days and accompanied his hosts to Sabbath services in the ground floor of the square, sturdy fort. One of the settlers beat a drum to call the others from their homes for the service. De Rasieres watched them gather in front of Captain Standish's house, the last one on the right going up the street to the fort. For the short walk up the hill, they formed a line of march, three abreast. In front marched a sergeant from Standish's small army. Behind him marched

Governor Bradford, with Elder Brewster on his right, and
Captain Standish on his left. The Governor wore a long
robe. The elder wore a long cloak, as did some of the
men. Captain Standish wore his side arms and carried a
cane. The others marched behind them "in good order,"
each man carrying a musket or firelock, which he set
down near him in the meeting house.

Although wilderness surrounded the stockade on three
sides, the Pilgrims conducted themselves with the formal
dignity characteristic of a church service in England or
Holland. The muskets at their sides were their only
recognition of the frontier.

De Rasieres eagerly reported on all the aspects of Plymouth life and the surrounding woods. "The savages
say that far in the interior there are certain beasts of
the size of oxen, having but one horn, which are very
fierce. The English have used great diligence in order
to see them, but cannot succeed therein, although they
have seen the flesh and hides of them which were
brought to them by the savages."

He was impressed by the settlers' good relationships
with the Indians, and by "the respect they from the very
first have established amongst them." Nevertheless,
there were those muskets beside them even in church,
and the stockade around the settlement.

Isaac Allerton made a second trip to England, returning with satisfactory news of further negotiations with
the Adventurers, as well as such supplies as shoes,
knives, shot and powder, hoes, spades, iron pots and
spices.

He also brought, without instructions from the church
at Plymouth, a minister who proved to be as great a
disappointment as Lyford had been. His name was Mr.

Rogers—first name unknown—and he turned out to be "crazed in his brain." The Pilgrims sent him back to England as soon as they could, and began to question the judgment of Isaac Allerton. Bradford wrote, "Mr. Allerton was much blamed that he would bring such a man over, they having charge enough otherwise." It was an unneeded expense to burden the poor colony with Rogers' transportation and living expenses.[35]

Some of the leaders, Bradford especially, were beginning to question some of Allerton's other actions, although they could hardly believe he would betray their faith in him. He began bringing some goods from England which he sold for his own private profit. On the next trip he brought still more, mixed in with the common store, and he was selling privately to nearby settlements. It soon became evident that Allerton was taking advantage of his public position. They were reluctant to accuse him. As Bradford said in Biblical terms, "Love thinks no evil nor is suspicious."[36]

The colony continued to use Allerton as their agent, and he sailed regularly between England and Plymouth.

The financial tangles between the Pilgrims and a series of backers in England persisted until 1646, due to a mixture of bad luck, poor accounting and sharp dealing on the part of the creditors. Allerton completed negotiations in 1626 whereby the Pilgrims "bought out" the Adventurers' interest for 1,800 pounds and borrowed that sum from other creditors, to be paid back over a period of time.

Several Pilgrim leaders formed a company known as "The Undertakers," which would take charge of the colony's trade for six years and in return would pay all the colony's debts. The first undertakers were Bradford, Allerton and Standish. They chose as partners William

Brewster, Edward Winslow, John Alden, John Howland
and Thomas Prence. Later four of the English Adventurers also became Undertakers.

The arrangement worked well at first, but within a
few years the Undertakers found themselves deeper in
debt, despite the quantity of furs and other goods they
had sent to England. Reluctant to suspect Allerton, they
were finally forced to the realization that he was playing
his own game. They probably would have acted sooner
if Brewster had not been Allerton's father-in-law.

Bradford wrote of Allerton, "Yea, he screwed up his
poor old father-in-law's account to above 200 pounds and
brought it on the general account, and to befriend him
made most of it to arise out of those goods taken up by
him at Bristol, at 50 percent, because he knew they
would never let it lie on the old man; when alas! he, poor
man, never dreamt of any such thing, nor that what he
had could arise near that value, but thought that many of
them had been freely bestowed on him and his children
by Mr. Allerton."[37]

Allerton continued on a dizzying financial course, conducting trade in competition with the Plymouth colony.
He was dismissed as the Undertakers' agent in about
1630, but he maintained a home in Plymouth for several
years. He also lost his post as the colony's Assistant
Governor, which he had held since 1621.[38]

In 1633 and 1634 an epidemic of infectious fever struck
the colony. Among its more than twenty victims were
both of the Brewster daughters, Patience Prence and
Fear Allerton.[39]

After Fear's death, Allerton, now the richest man in
the colony, left Plymouth for Marblehead to live with his
daughter, Remember, and her husband, Moses Maverick.
His other children remained in Plymouth. Isaac Allerton,

Jr., the only son born to Fear, was brought up by his Brewster relatives.[40]

Isaac Senior operated a fleet in Marblehead until Massachusetts authorities asked him to leave, probably at the urging of Plymouth leaders. He was briefly a merchant in New Amsterdam and finally settled in New Haven, where he lived in apparent prosperity. Upon his death in 1659 he left a large estate and many debts.

The 1633-34 epidemic also took one of Brewster's oldest friends, Samuel Fuller, the doctor and a deacon in the church. Fuller, one of the few early settlers to make a will, left "to old Mr. William Brewster my best hat and band." He added that he had never worn the hat.[41]

9 The Final Years

IN THE LAST SPRING of his life, William Brewster smoked his pipe packed with American tobacco and looked across the fertile acres of land he and his son tilled. They stretched to the waters of the bay where the *Mayflower* once sailed.

The ordered fields could have been English fields, and the grazing cattle made it an altogether English pastoral scene. The wilderness was gone here.[1] There were oxen to help work the fields, a red cow whose ancestors had once grazed English meadows, a steer, heifers, an unweaned calf, and some pigs.

Brewster was no longer living in the town of Plymouth, but in a new Plymouth colony settlement called Duxburrow (later Duxbury), where there was more and better land for farming. Duxburrow was about ten miles north of Plymouth town by a trail that led alongside the curve of the harbor, or a short crossing of the harbor by shallop.

The early years of privation were gone, and Brewster was enjoying the peace of a fruitful harvest. The cramped wattle and daub cottage was a memory, and Brewster's Duxburrow farm home was comfortable and spacious. He shared it with his son Love and Love's wife.

215

Brewster's 111 acres were located on a peninsula known as The Captain's Nook, where Captain Standish was the other principal land owner. Dorothy Wentworth, for many years Duxbury's town historian, points out that settlers in The Nook had the advantages of good springs, land cleared by the Indians, marshes with salt hay, and water on three sides.[2]

Little homey comforts were available now. Brewster slept on a feather bed in his sturdy bedstead, between sheets, with white blankets to keep out the cold. He had a desk where he might work and a green cushion to soften his chair. He liked green. There was a green rug, and sometimes he wore a green waistcoat or a pair of green drawers. On occasion he wore a violet-colored cloth coat or a pair of leather drawers or a blue suit, or he drew on his black silk stockings, still quite a luxury. Brewster had apparently hoped that a silk industry might be started in Plymouth colony; he had a book on growing silkworms, but New England's climate was not suitable.[3]

He had an assortment of headgear to cover his thinning hair from the winds off the bay—a lace cap, a quilted cap, a red one, a knitted cap and so on. He had a black hat and an old hat—perhaps one was the hat willed him by Dr. Fuller.[4]

Only a few of his things came with him on the *Mayflower*, probably his sword, rapier, dagger and knife and a pistol. And of course the earlier books in his extensive library, which eventually numbered about 400 books.

There were a few items of something like luxury—a silver beaker and a spoon, a pewter bottle, table cloths and a case for his tobacco.[5]

William Brewster's grandchildren were always in and out of the Duxburrow house. Love Brewster married Sarah Collier in 1634 and, as part of their marriage contract, William gave them the Duxburrow house, effective on his death. Sarah's father was William Collier, one of the Adventurers, who left his London brewery and moved his family to the Plymouth colony in 1633. The next year Collier was named Assistant Governor.

Love and Sarah Brewster had four children, and after the death of Fear Allerton, Love and Sarah—and William Brewster—brought up Fear's son, Isaac Allerton, Jr. Young Isaac must have shared his grandfather's interest in books; in 1650 he became the first student from Plymouth to be graduated from Harvard, the college founded in 1636.

Richard More continued to live with the Brewsters for a time. By 1637 he was the owner of 20 acres at nearby Eagle's Nest Point. The land is said to have been a gift from William Brewster to his former ward.[6]

In November 1637 More sold his Duxburrow property, and the following January he was granted one-half acre of land in Salem. He became a mariner and eventually a ship's captain.[7]

Across a little bridge over a creek which flowed through the meadow was the home of William's older son, Jonathan, and his wife, Lucretia. The Jonathan Brewsters had eight children. They were early residents of Duxburrow, but Jonathan later became the Pilgrims' resident agent at trading posts in Connecticut. His troublesome in-law, John Oldham, often made life difficult, at one point by opening a rival nearby post. Nevertheless Oldham finally made his peace with the Plymouth settlers and had liberty to come and go as he liked. Oldham was murdered by Indians in a quarrel on Block Island in 1636; his death touched off the Pequot War.

At Jonathan's trading post, now the site of Norwich, Conn., he set up a small laboratory for amateur chemical experiments. John Winthrop, Jr., Governor of Connecticut, had a similar lab. Winthrop and Jonathan Brewster compared results and both exchanged books with Gershom Bulkeley, a minister at Wethersfield, Conn.[8]

William Brewster's older daughter, Patience Prence, left five children when she died. Soon afterward, the widower Thomas Prence married Mary Collier, the sister of Love Brewster's wife Sarah. Thomas and Mary had four children. For several years the Prence family also lived in Duxburrow, later moving to Eastham on Cape Cod. Prence was elected Governor of Plymouth colony in 1634 and 1638—occasionally Bradford asked for a respite in his nearly life tenure as Governor. After Bradford's death, Prence was elected Governor in 1657, serving until his own death in 1673.

William Brewster's youngest son, Wrestling, died young, and the circumstances of his death are vague. Bradford wrote that Wrestling "died a young man unmarried."[9]

William Brewster's Duxburrow neighbors included many old friends from the Leyden and *Mayflower* days.

In a house overlooking the bay, on the land next to Brewster's, lived Captain Standish, still in charge of the colony's defense and frequently serving terms as Assistant Governor.

Nearby was the home of tall John Alden, the "hopeful young man" who signed on before the *Mayflower* sailed to care for the company's barrels; he and Priscilla were the parents of nine children.

George Soule, who came on the *Mayflower* as a servant of Edward Winslow, had his freedom and a farm in Duxburrow. Two who had been children during the Leyden days were now Duxburrow neighbors—Phillipe De La Noye (Delano, he was Franklin Delano Roosevelt's ancestor) and Moses Symonson (Simmons). Both came over on the *Fortune*.

So Brewster was surrounded in the last of his life by those who had worked with him to establish the colony. Despite the first winter and the later fever epidemic, many *Mayflower* passengers were still living twenty years later and acting as leaders in the little colony.

Only Bradford and Brewster's son Jonathan remained to share the memory of how it all started in Scrooby. Bradford still lived in the old town of Plymouth, and he mourned the departures of others by death or to the new settlements. The church, he wrote sadly in 1644, was "like an ancient mother grown old and forsaken of her children, though not in their affections yet in regard of their bodily presence and personal helpfulness . . ."[10]

To the end of his life William Brewster remained the revered elder of the church, the post he had undertaken in Leyden 34 years earlier.

The continuing hope for a suitable ordained preacher for Plymouth was for many years met only with disappointment. In 1629 the Reverend Ralph Smith, who had briefly served at Nantasket, asked to come to Plymouth. He was chosen as Plymouth's pastor, but he resigned seven years later. Bradford wrote, "This year Mr. Smith laid down his place of ministry, partly by his own willingness as thinking it too heavy a burthen, and partly by the desire and by the persuasion of others."[11]

Finally, the same year, the Pilgrims had a minister who satisfied them (at least until he left in 1654). He was John Rayner, a Cambridge University graduate, and Bradford called him "an able and a godly man."[12]

The brilliant Roger Williams was for a time the "teacher" in the Plymouth church. The people of Plymouth liked Williams and admired his forceful preaching, but they feared his radical ideas. Williams was a Cambridge graduate, who served during his youth as a confidential employee of Sir Edward Coke, the distinguished jurist. He took notes of the Star Chamber proceedings in shorthand and transcribed them for Coke.[13]

Later Williams became a preacher, but fled to America after incurring the anger of Bishop Laud. After brief stormy periods in Boston and Salem, Williams came to Plymouth for two years, where he assisted Reverend Smith. The colony did not pay him but provided him with a house and farm land. Williams engaged in trade with the Indians and learned their language well enough that "I could debate with them in a great measure in their own language."[14]

He raised the question of Pilgrim ownership of the Indian lands, objecting that neither the settlers nor the English King had made any payment for them. He also favored a more rigid church Separatism than did Brewster and the other Pilgrim leaders. When the church at Salem invited Williams to return to it, Brewster recommended his dismissal from Plymouth. Elder Brewster recalled the precarious period twenty years earlier when the church in Amsterdam was split over theological opinions. Roger Williams was a brilliant man, an eloquent preacher, but Brewster regarded him as a threat to the stability of the church.[15]

Williams eventually left Salem too and was banished in mid-winter from the Massachusetts Bay colony because of his increasingly radical ideas. He settled near Plymouth, but Edward Winslow, then Governor, urged him to move a little further on. Williams wrote later of Winslow's letter "lovingly advising me since I was fallen into the edge of their bounds and they were loathe to displease the Bay, to remove but to the other side of the water and then, he said, I had the country free before me and might be as free as themselves and we should be loving neighbors together."[16]

Williams finally settled in what became Providence, R.I., on land the Indians gave him in return for his services. He helped arrest and prosecute four Englishmen of Plymouth who robbed and murdered an Indian messenger near Providence in 1638. One accused murderer escaped before trial, but the other three were tried and convicted in a Plymouth court, with Williams giving evidence. The three Englishmen were executed in the presence of Williams and Indian friends of the murdered man.[17]

The settlers at Duxburrow found the trip to Plymouth long, especially in winter, and soon established a church in Duxburrow. Brewster served as its elder, in addition to his life-long post as elder of the Plymouth church. The Reverend Ralph Partridge, a capable and respected man, was minister at Duxburrow.

Plymouth colony remained small; there were only about 250 settlers by 1634. By 1643 the population reached 3,000 in the old town and its satellite communities. Other English settlements were growing up in many parts of New England. In a tremendous wave of immigration some 200 ships brought English settlers to New England between 1628 and 1640. By 1640 there were 16,000 people in the neighboring Massachusetts Bay colony.[18]

Plymouth and Duxburrow were almost backwaters now, but they experienced small changes. Duxburrow in 1638 organized an annual fair, the first in America, and Francis Sprague was licensed to open a tavern. A year later, a grist mill and a fulling mill for finishing homespun cloth were opened. A tract of Duxburrow land was set aside as a common where any farmer's marked cattle could be pastured.

The growth of new settlements necessitated further regulations. In 1636, Governor Bradford named a commission to draw up a formal code of laws for the colony. Brewster was a member of that commission.

Plymouth enjoyed a period of prosperity in providing agricultural goods for the Massachusetts Bay newcomers, exchanging them for the tools and cooking utensils which they often lacked. The Plymouth farmers sold cattle, timber, draft animals and foodstuffs, but by 1641 the immigration boom was over for a time, and Plymouth economy declined.[19]

Brewster lived on through all these changes. Bradford later wrote, "The Lord upheld him to a great age."[20]

There was more time now to enjoy reading the books in his growing library, although somehow he had always managed to find some time for books. So did Bradford, who studied Hebrew in his old age so that he might be able to read the language of many Bible books as they were written. Even the military man, Captain Standish, had a number of books, including a translation of the *Iliad.*

Brewster brought some of his books with him on the *Mayflower*, and he continued to add to his collection with shipments from England. The historian, Henry M. Dexter, said that at least a fourth of Brewster's books were published after 1620, and that "in only two of the years which the Elder spent in Plymouth before his last—namely 1639 and 1642—did he fail to avail himself of some of the freshest literature of the fatherland." He bought an English translation of *Seneca's Morals* from William Peirce, the friendly ship master who let Bradford copy the Lyford-Oldham letters.[21]

Over the years, William Brewster would always find time for books. What memories many held for him! John Robinson, the beloved Leyden pastor, wrote four of the books in his library. Brewster himself had published eleven of the volumes on the clandestine printing press in Choir Alley. In Brewster's collection was Bacon's book about the Earl of Essex, the young courtier whose career Brewster had followed from their schooldays at Cambridge until the execution of Essex. And John Smith's *Description of New England*. How they studied Smith's descriptions before they sailed for the New World!

There were a few "how to" books—the one on raising silkworms (impractical, sadly), prescribing medicine, or increasing timber production.

Brewster owned a tragedy called *Messalina* and a smattering of poetry but not a single line of Shakespeare.

The largest number of books consisted of works on theology, many in Latin.

On the flyleaves of some of his books, Brewster wrote a curious motto, *Hebel est omnis Adam*. It is a bilingual pun upon the names of Adam and Abel, partly translated into Latin from the Biblical Hebrew. Hebel (Abel) was the first man to die, and his death signifies the transitory nature of human beings. The name of Adam, his father, is also the Hebrew for all mankind. In the Pilgrims' Geneva Bible, the English translation of the verse is, "Man is like to vanitie: his daies are like a shadowe, that vanisheth." (Psalm 144:4.)[22]

Brewster's reflections on the illusory quality of vanity would have had their beginnings in the days of his youth. There were many examples. He remembered the Earl of Leicester riding in triumph through the Netherlands, and dying a few years later of illness on his way to a spa.

He remembered William Davison receiving the confidences of the Queen of England, only to be banished from her presence forever. And he remembered the rise and fall of the Earl of Essex.

He always especially pitied those who had once enjoyed good fortune and had lost it because of religious or capricious oppression. "And," Bradford wrote, "None did more offend and displease him than such as would haughtily and proudly carry and lift up themselves, being risen from nothing and having little else in them to commend them but a few fine clothes or a little riches more than others."[23]

Many thoughtful Elizabethans wrote about the danger of vanity; it was always at their elbow. Shakespeare in *As You Like It* has one of the characters say of the Forest of Arden, "Are not these woods more free from peril than the envious court?"[24]

Sir Walter Raleigh on the eve of his execution wrote to his wife, "If you can live free from want, care for no more; for the rest is but vanity."[25]

When the slow New England spring of 1644 was quickening the woods around the Plymouth colony, William Brewster's life was ebbing. The month was April.[26]

William Bradford was with Brewster at the last, as he had been with him through so much. Bradford describes Brewster's final hours:

"He was near fourscore years of age (if not all out) when he died. He had this blessing added by the Lord to all the rest; to die in his bed, in peace, amongst the midst of his friends, who mourned and wept over him and ministered what help and comfort they could unto him, and he again recomforted them whilst he could. His sickness was not long, and till the last day thereof he did not wholly keep his bed. His speech continued till somewhat more than half a day, and then failed him, and about nine or ten a clock that evening he died without any pangs at all. A few hours before, he drew his breath short, and some few minutes before his last, he drew his breath long as a man fallen into a sound sleep without any pangs or gaspings, and so sweetly departed this life into a better.''[27]

The pilgrim's journey was over.

APPENDIX A

The Mayflower Compact

In the Name of God, Amen. We whose names are underwritten, the loyal subjects of our dread sovereign Lord King James, by the Grace of God of Great Britain, France and Ireland King, Defender of the Faith, etc.

Having undertaken for the Glory of God, and advancement of the Christian faith, and honor of our King and Country, a voyage to plant the first Colony in the northern parts of Virginia, do by these presents solemnly and mutually in the presence of God and one of another, covenant and combine ourselves together into a civil body politic, for our better ordering and preservation, and furtherance of the ends aforesaid; and by virtue hereof to enact, constitute and frame such just and equal laws, ordinances, acts, constitutions, and offices, from time to time, as shall be thought most meet and convenient for the general good of the Colony, unto which we promise all due submission and obedience. In witness whereof we have hereunder subscribed our names at Cape Cod, the 11th of November, in the year of the reign of our Sovereign Lord King James, of England, France and Ireland the eighteenth, and of Scotland, the fifty-fourth. Anno Domini 1620.

APPENDIX B

The First Thanksgiving

The American tradition of Thanksgiving Day is based on this account in Edward Winslow's Dec. 11, 1621, letter to a London friend, printed in Mourt's Relation, *1622:*

Our harvest being gotten in, our Governor sent four men on fowling, that so we might after a more special manner rejoice together, after we had gathered the fruit of our labors; they four in one day killed as much fowl, as with a little help beside, served the company almost a week, at which time amongst other recreations, we exercised our arms, many of the Indians coming amongst us, and amongst the rest their greatest King Massasoit, with some 90 men, whom for three days we entertained and feasted, and they went out and killed five deer, which they brought to the Plantation and bestowed on our Governor and upon the Captain and others. And although it be not always so plentiful, as it was at this time with us, yet by the goodness of God, we are so far from want, that we often wish you partakers of our plenty.

Reference Notes

Complete information about sources is given in the bibliography.

Unless otherwise noted, all page numbers for Bradford refer to William Bradford's *Of Plymouth Plantation*, the Alfred A. Knopf edition edited by Samuel Eliot Morison and published as *Of Plymouth Plantation 1620-1647*. Unless otherwise noted, citations for Willison refer to George F. Willison's *Saints and Strangers*, and citations for Burgess refer to Walter H. Burgess's biography of John Robinson.

Because much information is based on English original documents and on books long out of print, secondary sources and reprints when available are cited. Many Pilgrim documents are excerpted in Willison's *The Pilgrim Reader*. Several original documents are reprinted in Alexander Young's *Chronicles of the Pilgrim Fathers of the Colony of Plymouth*. The 1844 edition of Young's book was reprinted in 1974 by the Genealogical Publishing Company.

One. DOWN THE GREAT NORTH ROAD TO LONDON

1. Burgess, p. 103; Harris and Jones, p. 18.
2. Willison, p. 14.
3. Unpublished notes of Walter H. Burgess, McLachlan Library, Unitarian College, Manchester, England.
4. Hunt, "The Mother of Elder William Brewster of the *Mayflower*," *New England Historical* and *Genealogical Register*, 124 (1970), p. 250. Mr. Hunt presents other relevant material in "New Light on the Brewsters of Scrooby and New England," *American Genealogist*, 41 (1965), p. 1, including the point that one 16th century document referred to William Brewster as "gen.," an abbreviation of the Latin *generosus*, or well born, a class distinction.
5. Ibid.
6. Brown, p. 49
7. Ibid, pp. 50-2.
8. Ibid, pp. 52-3.
9. Ibid.
10. Willison, p. 15.

Two. CAMBRIDGE
AND THE YOUNG RADICALS

1. Willison, p. 17.
2. Steegmann, pp. 53-5.
3. Ibid.
4. Rowse, pp. 501-4; Notestein, pp. 117-120.
5. See note 4.
6. Notestein, pp. 117-120.
7. Rowse, pp. 496, 501.
8. Ibid, p. 504.
9. Notestein, pp. 123, 125.
10. Ibid, p. 6
11. *Aubrey's Brief Lives*, University of Michigan edition, p. 174.
12. Notestein, p. 79.
13. Jenkins, *Elizabeth and Leicester*, p. 102.
14. Steegmann, pp. 19-20.
15. Ibid, pp. 21-2; Jenkins, *Elizabeth the Great*, pp. 105-7.
16. Thompson, p. 364; Bowen, *Francis Bacon*, p. 33.
17. *Tamburlaine the Great, Part I*, Act I, Scene II.
18. Willison, pp. 33-4.
19. Ibid, pp. 60-5.
20. Ibid.
21. Ibid.
22. Ibid, p. 33.
23. Ibid.
24. Notestein, p. 143.
25. Bradford, p. 325.

Three. THE COURT
OF THE GLORIOUS QUEEN

1. Notestein, p. 132; Wright and La-Mar, p. 364.
2. Jenkins, *Elizabeth and Leicester*, p. 222.
3. Nicolas, p. 11.
4. Bradford, p. 325.
5. Nicolas, p. 201.
6. Steele, pp. 81-3.
7. Nicolas, pp. 3-4.
8. Neale, p. 251.
9. Howard, p. 5.

10. Steele, pp. 105-6.
11. Ibid.
12. Froude, 10:6.
13. Ibid, pp. 3, 4.
14. Bradford, p. 325.
15. Read, *Mr. Secretary Walsingham and the Policy of Queen Elizabeth*, 1:325-6.
16. Nicolas, p. 8.
17. Read, *Walsingham*, 1:352.
18. Nicolas, p. 8.
19. Read, *Walsingham*, 3:82.
20. Motley, *History of United Netherlands*, 1:92.
21. Ibid, 1:311, 317.
22. Howard, p. 176.
23. Steele, p. 55.
24. Motley, *United Netherlands*, 1:334.
25. Read, *Lord Burghley and Queen Elizabeth*, p. 322.
26. Steele, p. 58.
27. Ibid, p. 59.
28. Bradford, p. 325.
29. Luke, p. 487.
30. Read, *Walsingham*, 3:115.
31. Luke, pp. 489-90.
32. Steele, pp. 62-7.
33. Motley, *United Netherlands*, 1:400.
34. Ibid.
35. Ibid, 1:413.
36. Steele, p. 72.
37. Nicolas, p. 20.
38. Jenkins, *Elizabeth and Leicester*, p. 312.
39. Froude, 12:170.
40. Ibid; Read, *Walsingham*, 3:137.
41. Froude, 12:170.
42. Motley, *United Netherlands*, 1:436; Waldman, p. 184.
43. Jenkins, *Elizabeth and Leicester*, p. 314.
44. Read, *Burghley*, p. 327.
45. Froude, 12:170.
46. Nicolas, p. 30.
47. Read, *The Government of England Under Elizabeth*, p. 7.
48. Nicolas, p. 38.
49. Fraser, pp. 475-6.

50. Ibid, p. 481.
51. Ibid, p. 482.
52. Ibid, pp. 482-3.
53. Ibid, pp. 488-9.
54. Read, *Burghley*, pp. 351-2.
55. Ibid, pp. 360-1.
56. Read, *Walsingham*, 3:54.
57. Ibid, p. 55.
58. Nicolas, p. 77.
59. Ibid, p. 78.
60. Jenkins, *Elizabeth and Leicester*, pp. 322, 330.
61. The account of the interview between Davison and the Queen appears in Nicolas, pp. 79-84.
62. Ibid.
63. Ibid, p. 86.
64. Ibid, pp. 88-92.
65. Ibid, pp. 92-4; Read, *Burghley*, pp. 368-9.
66. Nicolas, pp. 97-9.
67. Ibid, p. 99.
68. Ibid, pp. 100-102; Fraser, p. 329; Read, *Walsingham*, 3:64.
69. Nicolas, pp. 104-5, 169.
70. Ibid, pp. 114-5.
71. Froude, 12:346-7.
72. Nicolas, pp. 116-7.
73. Ibid, pp. 117-8; Read, *Burghley*, pp. 371-2.
74. Froude, 12:352; Read, *Burghley* p. 373.
75. Froude, 12:352, 357-8.
76. Read, *Government of England*, p. 16.
77. Read, *Burghley*, p. 351; Froude, 12:352, 353.
78. Nicolas's account of the trial, partly taken from Davison's manuscripts, appears on pp. 131-42, also p. 305; Froude, 12:351-5; Read, *Burghley*, p. 377.
79. See note 78.
80. Camden, University of Chicago Press edition, p. 295.
81. Read, *Burghley*, p. 374.
82. Luke, p. 557.
83. Adamson and Folland, p. 367.
84. Bradford, p. 327.

Four. THE MAKING OF A REBEL

1. Neale, pp. 297-8; Jenkins, *Elizabeth the Great*, p. 285.
2. Wernham, *English Historical Review*, Oct. 1931, p. 632, says a Spanish agent reported on Nov. 6 that Davison had been released. Records of the Constable's Office, Tower of London, state that Davison was imprisoned from 1587 to 1589. Read, *Burghley*, p. 575, says Burghley and Walsingham wrote on Oct. 23, 1588, to the Lieutenant of the Tower, directing him to release Davison secretly to the custody of Sir Robert Constable.
3. Steele, pp. 95-6; Nicolas, p. 172.
4. Wernham, p. 636.
5. Ibid, p. 632; Steele, p. 98.
6. Burgess unpublished notes.
7. Burgess, *Robinson*, p. 81.
8. Brown, pp. 59-61.
9. Ibid.
10. Ibid. (Cites *State Papers Domestic. Elizabeth*, Vol. ccxxxiii, 48. 22 August [1590], Sir John Stanhope to Sec. Davison); see also Hunt, *American Genealogist*, 41:2-3.
11. Brown, p. 63.
12. Burgess, p. 81.
13. Hunt, *American Genealogist*, 41:3-4.
14. Thompson, *The Bible in English 1525-1611*, pp. 193, 196.
15. Wright and Lamar, p. 256.
16. Steele, p. 110.
17. Notestein, p. 161.
18. Willison, p. 29.
19. Notestein, p. 117.
20. Bradford, p. 326.
21. Willison, p. 13.
22. Smith, *Bradford of Plymouth*, pp. 40-3; Young, p. 453.
23. See note 22; also Arber, p. 40.
24. Bradford, pp. 9-10. In 1648 in his *Dialogue*, Bradford wrote a brief biography of Clyfton; it is reprinted in Young, p. 453.
25. Smith, p. 53.

26. Bradford, p. 327.
27. Ibid, p. 3.
28. Brown, pp. 83-4; Willison, p. 49.
29. Brown, p. 79.
30. Bradford, p. 326.
31. Steele, p. 117.
32. Brown, p. 98.
33. Usher, p. 20.
34. Bradford, p. 12.
35. Ibid.
36. Usher, p. 28.
37. Bradford, p. 326; Brown, p. 102 3.
38. Brown, p. 98.
39. Ibid.
40. The episode is told in Bradford, pp. 12-15.
41. Ibid, p. 14.

Five. REFUGE IN THE LOWLANDS

1. Motley, *United Netherlands*, 4:551.
2. Jameson, p. 3.
3. Bradford, pp. 9, 16-17.
4. Willison, pp. 71-3.
5. Young, pp. 22, 450.
6. Quinn, pp. 344-357.
7. Willison, pp. 60-70.
8. Nicolas, p. 200.
9. Smith, p. 83.
10. Brown, pp. 120-1; Plooij, pp. 22-3.
11. See note 10.
12. Plooij, pp. 44-6.
13. Ibid.
14. Motley, *United Netherlands*, 4: 519, 523, 528, 533.
15. Bradford, p. 9; Willison, p. 80.
16. Bradford, p. 17.
17. Usher, pp. 33-6.
18. Bradford, p. 326.
19. Burgess, p. 102.
20. Ibid, p. 102.
21. Hunt, *N.E.H.&G.R.* 111:319.
22. Burgess, p. 103; Harris and Jones, p. 18.
23. See note 22.
24. Bradford, p. 16.

25. Ibid, p. 17.
26. Brown, p. 124; Burgess, p. 106.
27. Usher, pp. 42-3.
28. Bradford, pp. 18-19.
29. Plooij, pp. 48, 52.
30. Willison, p. 87.
31. Ibid, p. 82.
32. Bradford, Morison footnote, p. 444.
33. Smith, p. 85-7.
34. Ibid.
35. Ibid, p. 87.
36. Burgess, pp. 104, 107.
37. Willison, p. 444.
38. Clark, p. 195.
39. Willison, p. 94; Plooij, p. 57.
40. Plooij, pp. 32, 58-60; Burgess, p. 164.
41. Plooij, p. 58.
42. Ibid.
43. Harris and Jones, p. 30.
44. Burgess, p. 165; Plooij, p. 62.
45. Harris and Jones, p. 47.
46. Ibid, p. 63.
47. Willison, p. 96; Harris and Jones, p. 32.
48. Burgess, p. 166.
49. Ibid; *Proceedings*, Mass. Historical Society, March 1887, p. 269.
50. Plooij, p. 60; Harris and Jones, p. 20.
51. A good account of Carleton's search for the printer appears in Burgess, pp. 167-175.
52. Ibid.
53. Ibid.
54. Ibid.
55. Banks, pp. 38-9.
56. Steele, p. 117.
57. Burgess, pp. 167-175.
58. Plooij, p. 70.
59. Burgess, pp. 167-175.
60. Ibid.
61. Ibid, p. 170.
62. Ibid, p. 171.
63. Brown, pp. 165-6.
64. Willison, p. 100.
65. Burgess, p. 166.

Six. THE DREAM OF AMERICA

1. Smith, p. 107.
2. Raleigh's Works, vol. 8, *Guiana.*
3. Bradford, p. 28.
4. Bradford, p. 29, editor's footnote.
5. Willison, p. 106.
6. Bradford, pp. 356-7.
7. Ibid.
8. Banks, pp. 11-16.
9. The Seven Articles are summarized by Editor Morison in a footnote, Bradford, p. 31. They are reprinted in Brown, pp. 175-6; also in the Bradford 1912 edition edited by Ford, 1:72.
10. Bradford, pp. 31-2.
11. Ibid, 32-34.
12. Ibid, 19-20.
13. Ibid, p. 20.
14. Young, reprinting Edward Winslow's *Hypocrisie Unmasked*, p. 382; also Willison's *Pilgrim Reader*, pp. 56-7.
15. Petrie, pp. 58-9.
16. The correspondence and interview with Wolstenholme appear in full in Bradford, pp. 353-5.
17. Ibid.
18. Bradford, p. 30.
19. Ibid.
20. Harrison and Royston, p. 147.
21. Bradford, pp. 358-9.
22. Ibid, pp. 356-7.
23. Ibid.
24. Ibid, p. 358.
25. Smith, p. 103.
26. Bradford, p. 34, editor's footnote.
27. Ibid, p. 36.
28. Ibid, p. 360.
29. Smith, pp. 101, 110-1; Bradford, pp. 360, 362.
30. Bradford, p. 363.
31. Ibid, p. 43.
32. Ibid, p. 45.
33. Ibid.
34. Ibid, p. 375.
35. Ibid, pp. 47-8; *Hypocrisie Unmasked* in Young, p. 384; excerpts in Willison, *Pilgrim Reader*, pp. 74-5.
36. *Hypocrisie Unmasked*, see note 35.
37. Brown, pp. 191-3.
38. Young, p. 384.
39. Bradford, p. 47.

Seven. THE GREATEST ADVENTURE BEGINS

1. Bradford, pp. 368-71.
2. Ibid, pp. 54-7.
3. Ibid, pp. 53-4.
4. Descriptions of the passengers and crew appear in Banks, pp. 19-29, 44; Willison, pp. 121-3, 437-46; Usher, p. 69; Bradford, pp. 441-8; Stoddard, pp. 105-163.
5. Bradford, p. 443.
6. Ibid, p. 59; Harris and Jones, p. 45, suggest that the screw was part of the Leyden press.
7. Bradford, p. 58.
8. Willison, p. 443.
9. Ibid, pp. 139-41; Banks, pp. 61-4.
10. Bradford, p. 60, also see editor's note.
11. Bradford, p. 75.
12. Ibid, p. 62.
13. *Mourt's Relation*, p. 10. (This and many other passages of *Mourt's Relation* are reprinted in Willison, *Pilgrim Reader*.)
14. *Mourt's Relation*, p. 12, see editor's note.
15. The account is told in *Mourt's Relation*, pp. 18-27; also see note 13.
16. Ibid.
17. Ibid, pp. 52-4.
18. Ibid.
19. Bradford, pp. 72.
20. Willison, pp. 156-7; Smith, pp. 143-4; Willison, *Pilgrim Reader*, pp. 124-5 cites some of the notebook entries. The original notebook is now lost.
21. Bradford, p. 77.
22. See note 4 above.

Eight. LIFE IN THE FLOURISHING COLONY

1. Willison lists the *Fortune's* arrivals, p. 443-6.
2. Smith, pp. 159-60.
3. *Mourt's Relation*, p. 83; Willison, *Pilgrim Reader*, pp. 130-4.
4. Bradford, pp. 80-1.
5. Willison, *The Pilgrim Reader*, pp. 159-164, reprints most of Cushman's sermon.
6. Bradford, pp. 327-8.
7. Pory letter to Southampton appears in James, *Three Visitors to Early Plymouth*, pp. 5-13; in part in Willison, *Pilgrim Reader*, pp. 188-93; postscript to letter to Bradford, in Bradford, p. 113.
8. Bradford, p. 374-5.
9. Ibid, pp. 327-8.
10. Ibid, p. 144.
11. Ibid, p. 376.
12. Passengers on *Anne* and *Little James* are listed in Willison, pp. 446-50.
13. James, Altham letter, p. 29.
14. Ibid, p. 24.
15. Bradford, p. 132.
16. *Mayflower Descendant*, 1:8.
17. *Mayflower Descendant*, 30:5.
18. *N.E.H. and G.R.*, 111:242, notes by John G. Hunt.
19. The story of Oldham and Lyford is told in Bradford, pp. 147-69.
20. Ibid, pp. 376-7.
21. Ibid, p. 373.
22. See note 19.
23. See note 19.
24. See note 19.
25. See note 19.
26. Bradford, pp. 169-70, editor's footnote.
27. Ibid, pp. 179-80.
28. *Mayflower Descendant*, 1:149, 2:114; 30:97. Newman A. Hall, "The Children of Isaac Allerton," *Mayflower Quarterly*, 47:14-18.
29. Willison, p. 473.
30. Ibid, p. 101.
31. The Plymouth Registry of Deeds has an original drawing of the first street.
32. Smith, p. 265.
33. Brewster family notebook, *Mayflower Descendant*, 1:7.
34. A translation of De Rasieres letter in Jameson, *Narratives of New Netherland*; excerpts in Willison, *Pilgrim Reader*. A translation also in James. Descriptions of life in the colony appear in Rutman, Willison, Arber, Demos, Usher, Langdon, Smith and many others.
35. Bradford, pp. 210-11.
36. Ibid.
37. Ibid, pp. 240-44.
38. Willison, pp. 311, 456.
39. A letter from Massachusetts Bay Governor John Winthrop dated Dec. 12, 1634, to his son in London reported that the pestilent fever had taken both Mr. Prence's wife and Mr. Allerton's wife. (*Mayflower Descendant*, 30:5.) Thomas Prence was Governor of Plymouth at the time.
40. Sarah Allerton, mentioned in the 1627 division of cattle, may also have been a child of Isaac and Fear. Dr. Newman A. Hall suggests this possibility in *The Mayflower Quarterly*, 47:15. She apparently died young.
41. *Mayflower Descendant*, 1:27.

Nine. THE FINAL YEARS

1. Rutman, p. 19.
2. Wentworth, p. 26.
3. Inventory and settlement of estate, *Mayflower Descendant*, 3:15-30.
4. Ibid.
5. Ibid.
6. Wentworth, p. 31.
7. *Mayflower Families Through Five Generations*, vol. 2, p. 122.

8. Morison, p. 250.
9. Bradford, p. 444.
10. Ibid, p. 334.
11. Ibid, pp. 292-3.
12. Ibid.
13. Ernst, p. 25.
14. Ibid, p. 75.
15. Willison, *Pilgrim Reader*, p. 422, excerpts Nathaniel Morton's *New England Memoriall*.
16. Ernst, p. 160.
17. Ibid, pp. 202-3; Bradford, pp. 299-301.
18. Rutman, p. 13; Usher, p. 171.
19. Rutman, pp. 13-16.
20. Bradford, p. 324.
21. Mass. Historical Society *Proceedings*, Oct. 1889, p. 82. The books in Brewster's estate are listed in the *Proceedings*, March 1887, pp. 261-274. Dexter's analysis of the books appears in the *Proceedings* for October 1889, pp. 37-85.
22. For an explanation of the motto, I am indebted to the Rev. Dr. Peter Gomes, Plummer Professor of Christian Morals, Harvard University.
23. Bradford, p. 327.
24. *As You Like It*, Act II, Sc. 1.
25. Adamson and Folland, p. 363.
26. The Brewster notebook, published in part in *Mayflower Descendant*, 1:7, gives the date of death as April 10, 1644. Bradford, p. 324, tells of Brewster's death in the chapter headed "Anno Dom: 1643," but he probably wrote the chapter early in 1644. He prefaced his account, "I am to begin this year with that which was a matter of great sadness and mourning unto them all." The years then began on March 25. Bradford said that Brewster died "about the 18th of April." The estate inventory was taken in May 1644. (*Mayflower Descendant*, 3:15-30.)
27. Bradford, p. 324.

Bibliography

The single most important source for *Pilgrim* was William Bradford's history, *Of Plymouth Plantation*. It is published in many editions. The one most useful to me was *Of Plymouth Plantation 1620-1647*, edited by Samuel Eliot Morison (New York: Alfred A. Knopf, Inc., copyright 1952). Morison has used modern spelling without altering Bradford's words.

My favorite modern telling of the Pilgrim adventure is George F. Willison's *Saints and Strangers* (New York: Reynal & Hitchcock, 1945). It is complete, accurate and interesting.

This is a list of books and articles which I used in preparing *Pilgrim*, some for factual research, others to learn more about the times in which William Brewster lived. Most dates refer to the first publication. A few books published after the research for *Pilgrim* was completed are also included to help those doing further research.

Adamson, J.H., and Folland, H.F. *The Shepherd of the Ocean, Sir Walter Ralegh and his Times*. Boston: Gambit, 1969.

Anderson, Jay, and Deetz, James. "The Ethno-Gastronomy of Thanksgiving." *Saturday Review of Science*, Nov. 25, 1972, pp. 29-39.

Arber, Edward. *The Story of the Pilgrim Fathers 1606-1623 A.D.* London: Ward & Downey; Boston and New York: Houghton Mifflin, 1897.

Aubrey, John. *Aubrey's Brief Lives.* Edited from the original manuscripts and with a life of John Aubrey by Oliver Lawson Dick. Secker and Warburg, 1949; Ann Arbor: University of Michigan Press, 1957.

Banks, Charles Edward. *The English Ancestry and Homes of the Pilgrim Fathers*. Baltimore: Genealogical Publishing Co., 1929.

Bartlett, Robert. *The Faith of the Pilgrims*. New York: United Church Press, 1978.

Bartlett, Robert. *The Pilgrim Way*. New York: United Church Press, 1971. (Excellent detailed account.)

Benet, Stephen Vincent. *Western Star.* New York, Toronto: Farrar & Rinehart, 1943.

Bowen, Catherine Drinker. *Biography: The Craft and the Calling.* Boston: Atlantic Monthly Press; Little, Brown, 1969.

Bowen, Catherine Drinker. *Francis Bacon: The Temper of a Man.* Boston: Atlantic Montly Press; Little, Brown, 1963.

Bradford, William. *Of Plimoth Plantation.* Edited by Worthington C. Ford. 2 vol. Massachusetts Historical Society, 1912.

Bradford, William. *Of Plymouth Plantation 1620-1647.* Edited by Samuel Eliot Morison. New York: Alfred A. Knopf, 1952.

Brewster, Dorothy. *William Brewster of the Mayflower: Partial Portrait of a Pilgrim.* New York: New York University Press, 1971.

Bridenbaugh, Carl. *Vexed and Troubled Englishmen.* Oxford University Press, 1968.

Brown, John. *The Pilgrim Fathers of New England and their Puritan Successors.* New York, Chicago, Toronto: Fleming H. Revell, 1896.

Burgess, Walter H. *The Pastor of the Pilgrims, a Biography of John Robinson.* New York: Harcourt, Brace and Howe; London: Williams and Norgate; 1920.

Burgess, Walter H. Unpublished notes for anticipated biography of William Brewster, in McLachlan library of Unitarian College, Manchester, England.

Burton, Elizabeth. *The Pageant of Stuart England.* New York: Charles Scribner's Sons, 1962.

Caffrey, Kate. *The Mayflower.* New York: Stein and Day, 1974.

Camden, William. *The History of the Most Renowned and Victorious Princess Elizabeth Late Queen of England.* 1617. Selected chapters edited and with an introduction by Wallace T. MacCaffrey. Chicago and London: University of Chicago Press, 1970.

Cecil, David. *The Cecils of Hatfield House.* Boston: Houghton Mifflin, 1973.

Chute, Marchette. *Shakespeare of London.* New York: E.P. Dutton, 1949.

Colby, Jean Poindexter. *Plimoth Plantation Then and Now.* New York: Hastings House, 1970.

Cowie, Leonard W. *The Pilgrim Fathers.* London: Wayland, 1970. New York: G.P. Putnam's Sons, 1972.

Deetz, James. *In Small Things Forgotten.* Garden City, N.Y.: Doubleday, 1977.

Demos, John. *A Little Commonwealth.* New York: Oxford University Press, 1970.

Dexter, Henry Martyn. *The England and Holland of the Pilgrims.* Boston: Houghton Mifflin, 1905.

Dillon, Francis. *The Pilgrims.* Garden City, N.Y.: Doubleday, 1975.

Dodd, A.H. *Life in Elizabethan England.* New York: G.P. Putnam's Sons, 1961.

Ernst, James. *Roger Williams, New England Firebrand.* New York: Macmillan, 1932.

Fraser, Antonia. *Mary Queen of Scots.* England: Weidenfeld & Nicolson, 1969. New York: Delacorte Press, 1969.

Froude, James Anthony. *History of England from the Fall of Wolsey to the Death of Elizabeth.* 12 vols. London, 1862-70. New York: Reprinted by AMS Press, 1969.

Gill, Crispin. *Mayflower Remembered.* New York: Taplinger, 1970.

Goodwin, John A. *The Pilgrim Republic.* Boston: Houghton Mifflin, 1920.

Harris, Rendel, and Jones, Stephen K. *The Pilgrim Press.* Cambridge: W. Heffner & Sons, 1922.

Harrison, Molly, and Royston, O.M. *How They Lived*, vol. 2. An Anthology of original accounts written between 1485 and 1700. Oxford: Basil Blackwell, 1963.

Hodges, Margaret. *Hopkins of the Mayflower: Portrait of a Dissenter.* New York: Farrar, Straus & Giroux, 1972.

Holisher, Desider. *Pilgrims Path.* New York: Stephen-Paul, 1947.

Holloway, Naomi D. *Pedigree of Mary Wentworth.* Boulder, Colo.: Naomi D. Holloway, 1969.

Howard, Philip. *The Royal Palaces.* Boston: Gambit, 1970.

Hunt, John G. "New Light on the Brewsters of Scrooby and New England." *American Genealogist*, vol. 41 (1965)

Hunt, John G. "The Mother of Elder William Brewster of the

Mayflower." *New England Historical and Genealogical Register,* vol. 124 (1970).

Hunt, John G. "Notes on Brewster-Oldham line; also on identity of Robert and Ann Peck," *N.E.H.&G. Register,* vol. 111 (1957).

Hunter, Joseph. *Collections Concerning the Church or Congregation of Protestant Separatists formed at Scrooby.* London, 1854.

James, Sydney V. Jr. Editor of *Three Visitors to Early Plymouth.* Letters by John Pory, Emmanuel Altham and Isaack De Rasieres. Plymouth: Plimoth Plantation, 1963.

Jameson, J. Franklin. *Narratives of New Netherland 1609-1664.* New York: Charles Scribner's Sons, 1909; reprinted by Barnes & Noble, 1959.

Jenkins, Elizabeth. *Elizabeth The Great.* New York: Coward-McCann, 1959.

Jenkins, Elizabeth. *Elizabeth and Leicester.* New York: Coward-McCann, 1962.

Langdon, George D. Jr. *Pilgrim Colony, A History of New Plymouth.* New Haven and London: Yale University Press 1966.

Luke, Mary M. *Gloriana, the Years of Elizabeth I.* New York: Coward, McCann & Geoghegan, 1973. Toronto: Longman Canada 1973.

Massachusetts Historical Society *Proceedings,* March 1887 and October 1889, on Elder Brewster's library.

The Mayflower Descendant (Periodical issued by the General Society of Mayflower Descendants), particularly vols. 1 and 3.

Mayflower Families Through Five Generations, Plymouth, Mass.: General Society of Mayflower Descendants. Vol. 1, *Francis Eaton,* by Lee D. van Antwerp; *Samuel Fuller,* by Arthur H. and Katharine W. Radasch; *William White,* by Robert M. Sherman and Ruth W. Sherman, edited by Lucy Mary Kellogg, 1975. Vol. 2, *James Chilton,* by Robert M. Sherman and Verle D. Vincent; *Richard More,* by Robert S. Wakefield and Lydia R.D. Finlay; *Thomas Rogers,* by Alice W.A. Westgate; edited by Robert M. Sherman, 1978. Vol. 3, *Descendants of George Soule,* by John Soule and

Milton E. Terry; edited by Anne Borden Harding, 1980. Vol. 4, *Elder William Brewster*, by Katharine Richardson Greeley, edited by Anne Borden Harding, was in preparation when *Pilgrim* was being readied for the printer.

The Mayflower Quarterly. (Periodical currently issued by the General Society of Mayflower Descendants.)

Morison, Samuel Eliot. *The Intellectual Life of Colonial New England*. New York: New York University, 1936. Ithaca and London: Cornell University Press, 1960.

Morley, Frank. *The Great North Road*. New York: Macmillan, 1961.

Motley, John Lothrop. *History of the United Netherlands from the Death of William the Silent to the Twelve Years' Truce— 1609*. 4 vol. New York: Harper & Brothers, 1867.

Motley, John Lothrop. *The Works of John Lothrop Motley*. 17 vol. New York and London: Harper, 1900.

Mourt, G. (pseud. for William Bradford and Edward Winslow) *A Relation, or Journal of the Plantation at Plymouth*. London: 1622. Ann Arbor: Facsimile produced by Xerox, University Microfilms, 1975.

Neale, J.E. *Queen Elizabeth I*. London, 1934. London: Jonathan Cape (paperback edition), 1967.

Nicolas, Nicholas H. *Life of William Davison*. London, 1823.

Notestein, Wallace. *1603-1630 The English People on the Eve of Colonization*. New York: Harper & Row, 1954.

Plooij, Daniel. *The Pilgrim Fathers from a Dutch Point of View*. New York: New York University Press, 1932.

Quinn, David Beers. *England and the Discovery of America 1481-1620*. New York: Alfred A. Knopf, 1974.

Read, Conyers. *The Government of England Under Elizabeth*. Washington: Folger Shakespeare Library, 1960.

Read, Conyers. *Lord Burghley and Queen Elizabeth*. Oxford: Alden Press; New York: Alfred A. Knopf, 1960.

Read, Conyers. *Mr. Secretary Cecil and Queen Elizabeth*. Great Britain: 1955. New York: Alfred A. Knopf, 1955. London: Jonathan Cape (paperback edition), 1965.

Read, Conyers. *Mr. Secretary Walsingham and the Policy of Queen Elizabeth*. 3 vol. Cambridge: Harvard University

Press; Oxford: Clarendon Press, 1925.

Rowen, Herbert H. *A History of Early Modern Europe 1500-1815.* New York: Holt, Rinehart & Winston, 1962.

Rowse, A.L. *The England of Elizabeth.* New York: Macmillan, 1950.

Rutman, Darrett B. *Husbandmen of Plymouth.* Boston: Beacon Press for Plimoth Plantation, 1967.

Sherman, Ruth Wilder. "The More Myth." *The Mayflower Quarterly,* vol. 38 (1972).

Sitwell, Edith. *The Queens and the Hive.* Boston, Toronto: Little, Brown, 1962.

Smith, Bradford. *Bradford of Plymouth.* Philadelphia and New York: J.B. Lippincott Company, 1951.

Steegmann, John. *Cambridge.* London, New York, Toronto, Sydney: B.T. Batsford Ltd., 1940.

Steele, Ashbel. *Chief of the Pilgrims: or the Life and Time of William Brewster.* Philadelphia: J.B. Lippincott and Co., 1857.

Stoddard, Francis R. *The Truth About the Pilgrims.* New York: Society of Mayflower Descendants in the State of New York, 1952. Baltimore: Republished by the Genealogical Publishing Co., 1976.

Strachey, Lytton. *Elizabeth and Essex.* New York: Harcourt, Brace, 1928.

Sumner, George. "Memoirs of the Pilgrim at Leyden." Boston: *Collections* of the Massachusetts Historical Society, vol. 9 of third series, 1846.

Thompson, Craig R. *The Bible in English 1525-1611.* Ithaca: Cornell University Press, 1958.

Thompson, Craig R. *Universities in Tudor England.* Ithaca: Cornell University Press, 1959.

Usher, Roland G. *The Pilgrims and their History.* New York: Macmillan, 1918.

Wagner, Anthony. "The Royal Descent of a Mayflower Passenger." *N.E.H.&G. Register,* vol. 85 (1970).

Wagner, Anthony. "The Origin of the Mayflower Children: Jasper, Richard and Ellen More." *N.E.H.&G. Register,* vol. 114 (1960).

Waldman, Milton. *Elizabeth and Leicester.* Boston: Houghton, Mifflin, 1945.

Wentworth, Dorothy. *Settlement and Growth of Duxbury 1628-1870.* Duxbury Rural and Historical Society, 1973.

Wernham, R.B. "The Disgrace of William Davison." *English Historical Review,* October 1931.

Williamson, Hugh Ross. *Kind Kit. An Informal Biography of Christopher Marlowe.* New York: St. Martin's, 1972.

Willison, George F. *The Pilgrim Reader. The Story of the Pilgrims as Told by Themselves and Their Contemporaries Friendly and Unfriendly.* Garden City, N.Y. Doubleday 1953.

Willison, George F. *Saints and Strangers.* New York: Reynal & Hitchcock, 1945.

Winslow, Edward. *Hypocrisie Unmasked.* London, 1646. New York: Reprinted from the original, Burt Franklin, 1968.

Wright, Louis B., and LaMar, Virginia A., Editors. *Life and Letters in Tudor and Stuart England.* Ithaca: Published for the Folger Shakespeare Library by Cornell University Press, 1962.

Young, Alexander. *Chronicles of the Pilgrim Fathers of the Colony of Plymouth.* Reprints many original Pilgrim documents. Boston: Little Brown, 1844. Baltimore: Reprinted by Genealogical Publishing Co. 1974.

Ziff, Larzer. *Puritanism in America.* New York: Viking, 1973.

Index

Acknowledgments

When he wrote about William Brewster's life, William Bradford wondered briefly "if to say a little were not worse than to be silent." The same question applies in acknowledging the help given me in preparing this book.

I did most of my research in the Library of Congress, but I also used the D.A.R. and National Genealogical Society Libraries in Washington, D.C., as well as the Fairfax County, Va., Public Library; the Mary Riley Styles Public Library in Falls Church, Va.; and the Martin Luther King Memorial Library in Washington, D.C. I did research in Plymouth, Mass., and in Scrooby, Manchester, Cambridge and London, England. People in all those places were helpful.

Many students of Pilgrim history are informed and inspired by the work of the Pilgrim Society and of Plimoth Plantation in Plymouth, Mass. Both contributed illustrations for this book, and I found the results of their ongoing research to be most helpful. The Art and Reference Division, Office of the Architect of the Capitol, made possible the publication in this book of a new mural which depicts the signing of the Mayflower Compact, in addition to other Pilgrim representations in the U.S. Capitol.

The sources of other illustrations are acknowledged in accompanying credit lines. I appreciate the courtesy of those who furnished the illustrations and authorized their publication.

I am indebted to many others who have made suggestions and encouraged me to publish *Pilgrim*. Dr. Jordan D. Fiore, Director of the Division of Social Sciences, Bridgewater Mass. State College, and an authority on Pilgrim history, read the book in manuscript and urged its publication. Mrs. Elsie B. Williams, a former assistant editor of the *Mayflower Quarterly*, also read the manuscript and made useful suggestions.

Many members of the General Society of Mayflower Descendants and the Elder William Brewster Society have expressed their interest. I have especially appreciated the encouragement of Stannard M. Butler, of the Albany, N.Y., Colony, Society of Mayflower Descendants.

Genealogist John G. Hunt has given me helpful insight into the ancestry and family of William Brewster and permission to use copyrighted material and unpublished research. I also appreciate permission to quote from the following:

Of Plymouth Plantation 1620–1647, by William Bradford. Edited by Samuel Eliot Morison. © 1952 by Alfred A. Knopf, Inc. Reprinted by permission of the publisher.

Saints and Strangers, by George F. Willison. © 1945 by Reynal & Hitchcock. Reprinted by permission of Florence H. Willison.

Three Visitors to Early Plymouth, edited by Sydney V. James, Jr. © 1963 by Plimoth Plantation. Reprinted by permission of the publisher.

The English People on the Eve of Colonization 1603–1630, by Wallace Notestein. © 1954 by Harper & Row, Publishers Inc. Adapted pp. 20, 21, 22, 26, 30, 91. Reprinted by permission of the publisher.

My husband, Robert B. Sherwood, shared in the development of *Pilgrim*, from the early years when we were retracing Brewster's travels to final editing of the manuscript, and has contributed in more ways than I could possibly mention.

M.B.S.

Colophon

Consulting by Kevin Osborn, and typesetting and paste-up by Barbara Shaw, at The Writer's Center, Glen Echo, Md. The type face used throughout the book is Compugraphic's Century Old Style; the text was set 11 on 13.5.

Offset printing and binding by McNaughton & Gunn, Ann Arbor,